The
UNIVERSITIES
we need

The
UNIVERSITIES
we need

Higher Education after Dearing

Nigel Blake • Richard Smith • Paul Standish

**KOGAN
PAGE**

YOURS TO HAVE AND TO HOLD

BUT NOT TO COPY

First published in 1998

Apart from any fair dealing for the purposes of research or private study, or criticism or review, as permitted under the Copyright, Designs and Patents Act 1988, this publication may only be reproduced, stored or transmitted, in any form or by any means, with the prior permission in writing of the publishers, or in the case of reprographic reproduction in accordance with the terms and licences issued by the CLA. Enquiries concerning reproduction outside these terms should be sent to the publishers at the undermentioned address:

Kogan Page Limited
120 Pentonville Road
London
N1 9JN
UK

Stylus Publishing Inc.
22883 Quicksilver Drive
Sterling
VA 20166-2012
USA

© Nigel Blake, Richard Smith and Paul Standish, 1998

The right of Nigel Blake, Richard Smith and Paul Standish to be identified as the authors of this work has been asserted by them in accordance with the Copyright, Designs and Patents Act 1988.

British Library Cataloguing in Publication Data

A CIP record for this book is available from the British Library.

ISBN 0 7494 2725 6

Typeset by Kogan Page
Printed and bound by Biddles Ltd, Guildford and King's Lynn.

Contents

Introduction: Reading Dearing

The Dearing Report – the report of The National Committee of Inquiry into Higher Education – was submitted to the Secretaries of State for Education and Employment, Wales, Scotland and Northern Ireland in July 1997. Widely publicized beforehand, it has since then generated much discussion and an extensive secondary literature. This book is in one sense a response to Dearing, and in places we analyse the Report in a degree of detail, questioning its assumptions and evaluating its recommendations. In another sense this book is about the future of higher education in the UK more broadly. It is already a commonplace that 'things have moved on' since Dearing, that Dearing was *then*, and this is *now*. The Kennedy and Fryer Reports are sometimes claimed to be more significant than the Dearing Report itself; the Green Paper, *The Learning Age*, sets out a view of lifelong learning, of the continuous acquisition of knowledge and skills and of work-based learning, that could revolutionize post-compulsory education in the UK more radically than anything to be found in Dearing. It is our intention to contribute to this broader debate: in this, our critique of Dearing is to be read more as critique of widespread underlying assumptions about higher education – ones which of course surface in Dearing, as in other recent reports and publications – than as critique of just one particular report which may before long come to seem of merely historical significance.

But already we begin to notice something about the elusiveness of debate here. Dearing, with its five Appendices and 14 Reports, amounts to over 1700 pages. The sheer scale of the thing threatens to defeat intelligent reading and analysis in a number of ways. First, there is the aspiration to comprehensiveness: there is a sense that, somewhere or another in Dearing, *everything* is said, all points of view are given their due: that whatever criticism might be offered, somewhere an obscure paragraph has probably taken account of it. Secondly, it becomes inevitable that it is the summary report that most people will read. In that characteristic feature of our age, the list – often italicized, bullet-pointed and decimally-numbered – signals what we busy people really need to remember. The result is that our thinking is thus done for us. Thirdly, these devices seldom register detailed argument or subtlety of thought, and so nothing that it is possible to take issue with in any interesting way. The language is bafflingly reasonable: it has the glossy smoothness office, where we try to walk and cannot gain any purchase. And fourthly, one senses an oscillation between the detail and the broader implicit message. If the critic finds fault with the detail, then she is losing sight of the larger view; if she calls this into question then she is over-looking the need for managerial precision, for answering questions of the form 'How exactly will you fund and deliver it?'

If everything is continually being superseded, of course, then it is point-less to offer analysis of what are always yesterday's reports and publica-tions. The pace of change, and the relentless assertion of the inevitability of change, create a climate in which to stop for thought[1] begins to look like economic treason. Consider the opening paragraph of *The Learning Age*:

> 1. We are in a new age – the age of information and of global competi-tion. Familiar certainties and old ways of doing things are disappear-ing. The types of jobs we do have changed as have the industries in which we work and the skills they need. At the same time, new oppor-tunities are opening up as we see the potential of new technologies to change our lives for the better. We have no choice but to prepare for this new age in which the key to success will be the continuous educa-tion and development of the human mind and imagination.

The imperative, starkly put ('We have no choice' – there is no alternative after all), is to keep moving, to be alert for the next opportunity, the next document with its bullet-points: to love Change as people in other cul-tures have been told to love the Party or the Army. The reader may be familiar with the kind of article, or management presentation, that begins with the solemn assertion: 'In an era of change, the only thing certain is change itself'. Nostrums about the importance of the manage-ment of change quickly follow, insisting that since all is in flux substance can be ignored and more power given to managers immediately.

The other familiar assertion in the paragraph above is that of globaliza-tion: that we are in an age of global competition. If there is any broad message that emerges from all the recent reports and official publica-tions on post-compulsory education it is this. In the face of the howling gale of international reconstruction of a global economy, in which foot-loose money has no inherent commitment to one society rather than any other, any insistence on the priority of any values over and above the vocational is implicitly represented as hopelessly naïve. Talk of intrinsic value and the role of higher education in sustaining a culture and social norms is all very well if we can still afford it; but unless we attend to the economy first, nothing is possible. The risk of failure in the globalized economy brings the prospect of absolute economic decline, a decline that will take culture and civilization down with it.

In what follows below we return to this broad message in a number of ways. The economic collapse, in the summer of 1997, of the 'tiger' economies of East Asia, reminds us that education alone will be no defence against economic disaster (the education systems of Japan, Taiwan and so on having been held up to us as models on numerous occasions). It is possible too even to question the relationship between economic strength and education (although to do so has become effectively another heresy). The determining consideration for international capital as it relocates is undoubtedly cost – labour costs, environmental costs, regulatory or tax costs. Levels of educational attainment are never more than one element in a complex array. And if this is so, and non-economic requirements on education are legitimate, then one may reasonably ask that the whole weight of a survival strategy should not be placed on education, and that education's other purposes should be given their due as well.

But the implications go deeper than this. The sudden East Asian economic collapse indicates only too vividly the sheer uncertainty of the global economy and its implications for national policy. The contemporary context for policy is not one of risk, in which at least probabilities, if not certainties, can be assigned to outcomes. Rather, governments now face a radical degree of uncertainty in which not even probabilities of success can be assigned. The very context of policy changes unpredictably. As Gray (1998) has recently reminded us, governments do not even know whether their policies will prove merely costly or outright unworkable. Yet it is precisely this kind of double-guessing of the unknowable that the Dearing Report attempts. Its cosily journalistic conception of globalization pre-empts consideration of the future of higher education in any context of serious economic debate. It does not attempt to raise the question whether there is some more reasonable response to this world of comprehensive uncertainty than to attempt to gamble in it and win. The argument from the inevitability of change proves, inconveniently, too powerful in the end.

Of course, this is all the more difficult to see where the hegemony of instrumental reason is assumed, and, as we shall show, this is clearly the case in the current policy documents and debate. One of the established roles of higher education that is being marginalized is its role in the transformation of individuals and of their understanding of their world. The role is being pushed to one side, if not abolished, by the new emphasis on a need for flexibility in graduates, whether graduates of universities or any other form of tertiary education or training. One implication of the new globalized economy, dancing to the new tunes of ever-accelerating change, is held to be that we should all be able and willing to constantly retrain. This is assumed to involve jumping from one set of skills to another, with the former left to rot if they are no longer needed. Knowledge and understanding, so important in the transformative role of higher education, begin to be thought of as mere encumbrances, assumed vulnerable to rapid obsolescence or reducible to the kind of information that can be encoded and stored on disk. Skills are the thing.

This is not a picture that asks for the transformation of students into flexible mathematicians, flexible linguists or flexible social scientists. On the contrary, it calls for graduates to be ideally no particular kind of person at all. The ideal graduate is not assumed, in this picture, to be one who can draw on her deep knowledge and understanding of one area of knowledge to extend it, sideways or in depth, or by analogy or reapplication to new areas. Unencumbered by bodies of knowledge, she becomes the adept of information access and the dubious beneficiary of 'transferable skills'. These in turn are not even the specific and sophisticated skills of, for instance, particular kinds of mathematical, linguistic or scientific work, but preferably skills as abstract, and as little linked to specific disciplines, as possible, the better to be 'transferred': communication skills, teamwork skills, personal skills and analytical skills – and, of course (Dearing: 9.17), the skills of learning how to learn. There are two problems with 'skills' conceived on such a general and abstract level. The first is that the very idea of transferable skills of such a kind is dubious; the second is that the mantra of skills – 'skills-talk' as we call it below – drowns out any talk of rationality, of criticism, of knowledge and understanding, conceived in any but the most instrumental way. Was ever a long-term management strategy for a whole economy built on flimsier grounds?

What kind of citizenship is implicitly offered to the bearer of these illusory skills, the subject of this empty form of flexibility? In effect the state (Blairite no less than Thatcherite) says to the citizen, 'As far as the economy goes, we don't really care just what kind of person you are. In fact, we would rather you were no one in particular, otherwise you will be less flexible'. What this adds up to is a picture of the citizen who is conceived by the State either as a redeployable cipher or an individualistic nuisance. As a programme of citizenship for the future, this lacks appeal, at best. But properly we should say it is ethically bankrupt, and it leaves us with a conception of the individual that is worryingly thin.

Dearing clearly seeks to democratize: what could be more democratic than the total accessibility and searchability of the Report on the World Wide Web? But what is the nature of this democracy? For the more these matters are understood in purely economic terms the less readily can be remembered the relation between universities and the culture which it is, arguably, their role to sustain and criticize. Of course, talk of 'culture' will sound alarm bells with some, and much more needs to be said about what that amounts to. And there is a shadow side to this point: the Dearing report does indeed sustain a certain culture of its own, but this is an educational culture that is seriously depleted, as this book will progressively show.

We have lost, to our detriment, certain ways of talking about teaching and learning. There is a need to reinstate a richer language. We are presented with a certain sort of vision: wider participation in a unified system; a de-differentiating of institutions where all universities can offer everything; transparency and commensurability through modularization and systems for credit accumulation and transfer, with student achievement properly recognized in clear Progress Files (Dearing: Recommendation 20); and, of course, the full exploitation of Communications and Information Technology. But in this 'vision' it is as if the sense of what a university is for has fallen off the edge. A portfolio of bits and bobs replaces any sense of an institution that could arouse a student's loyalty. But loyalty of a more important kind may disappear also – loyalty to a tradition of enquiry, to the courses that sustain such a tradition, and the kind of commitment that is at the heart of academic endeavour. Without this loyalty and commitment, we cannot but dilute the critical business that is at the heart of higher education. For critique is not mere cultural 'stroppiness' nor is it just academic fun – some immature nostalgia for 1968. It involves 'sticking with' the detailed, sometimes frustrating demands of an intellectual discipline which we see nonetheless as worth the effort. It is through commitment to critique of established knowledge that academic disciplines make progress and that the growth of knowledge is sustained, in science, technology and the professions no less than the humanities and social sciences. And it is the growth of knowledge that fuels the modern growth economy. In the

5

face of official panic at the prospect of industrial production moving elsewhere, and drawing on others' 'new skills', it is being forgotten that it will also move on in terms of the knowledge and understanding which inform its innovations – knowledge and understanding which can only be cultivated in traditions, albeit self-critical traditions. We destroy these traditions in our own country at our peril. The prospect, if we do so, is of a new subsidiary status in the world, not as players in the front line but as intellectual, academic and economic 'client states'. The real business of innovation will have moved elsewhere – ever so flexible as our workforce of educational peons may become. For peonage – day-labouring – is the pattern of future employment on which so much educational reform is almost explicitly predicated.

And, of course, the peons are now expected to pay for the privilege of any work worth doing at all. In the media coverage of Dearing and in political debate on higher education it is of course the issue of tuition fees that has secured most attention. Concentration on means, however – here literally the question of whose are the means to pay for higher education – has obscured the fact that Dearing devotes little space to proper discussion of ends. What universities are for, what the purpose or purposes of higher education might be, is not an issue pursued with any rigour or to any depth: one more sign, we would say, of the hegemony of instrumental reason, the dominance of questions of means over all other questions. Yet it is possible to imagine some impatience with our assertion here (although we attempt to substantiate it in some detail below). Here we have the most comprehensive report on higher education ever, with an entire chapter (Chapter 5) devoted to 'Aims and purposes'. How can we complain that Dearing has not discussed the aims of higher education? One answer is that if Dearing had done so, debate would have been stimulated on that very issue, in the way that debate was stimulated by J H Newman's publication of *The Idea of the University*, or more recently by Allan Bloom's *The Closing of the American Mind*. Dearing is hardly to be read with the same excitement. This is less to complain about this Report, than about the way in which such reports and other official publications, especially on education, have become a kind of substitute literature, their discursive form such that critical discussion is foreclosed by the format – the lists, the comprehensiveness, the inclusivity, the acknowledgement of disagreement which draws its sting and reduces diversity to an unexceptionable blandness.

This is the context in which we have tried to challenge the emerging consensus, to recover a more vigorous and more responsive language in which to discuss higher education. We write as philosophers of education, with broad experience in schools, in further and higher education; of undergraduate, postgraduate, adult continuing education and work-based learning. We have written this book in no conservative spirit, but in the belief that higher education is richer and more complex, and has more to offer its students, and their country and communities, than the terms of current debate would suggest.

Notes

1. The difficulty, and the importance, of thinking properly about education is a central theme of our recent book *Thinking Again: Education after Postmodernism* (Blake *et al*, 1998). In this we examine in greater depth the consequences of the prevalent language of education and the characteristic performativity of its systems.

1

Tuition Fees, Stakeholding and Citizenship

For a long time, higher education in the UK has been radically under-funded in all of its functions. It is, of course, a particular scandal that the Major Government expanded student numbers vastly whilst refusing to stump up anywhere near a commensurate increase in funding, thus reducing funding per head by 25 per cent since 1989.[1] Deep cuts and casualization of labour in the universities indicate that these reductions are not compatible with maintaining standards. So the proposition that new funds are needed goes without question. And the further proposition, that new funding should be raised disproportionately from those who enjoy most material success in our society, is a platitude of a modern democratic commitment to progressive taxation (a commitment so deep that the New Right succeeded only in eroding but never in abandoning it).

The social democratic instinct in such a situation would be unambiguous. New funds must be found by raising taxation, and this burden should fall mainly on the better off, simply because they *are* better off. So why has this idea been viewed as simply defunct for several years now? Why, in particular, are some funds to be recouped from students on the basis of repayable loans for tuition fees? Why is the social democratic instinct wrong?

It might seem that nobody (who 'matters') really believes that it is morally wrong, but simply that we all bow to the politically inevitable in a post-Thatcherite world, accepting necessary evils as more necessary than ever. Rare attempts to set out a genuine moral case for charging for tuition are instructive in their failure. Consider the attempt of David Robertson, a leading apologist for redistribution of funds for tertiary education by market-oriented means (Robertson, 1996). Robertson wants to argue for both increased participation and equalization of opportunities for 'lifelong learning', conceived as educationally neutral between university education and industrial training, and everything in between. These aims he clearly sees as morally compelling, no less than politically and economically necessary.

His first argument is that 'learning opportunities are invariably rationed by their affordability to public funds – and we cannot afford to ration the development of human potential this way' (Robertson, 1996: 154). But what then follows is in effect an argument in favour of rationing those opportunities instead by their affordability to private funds and employer sponsorship. Robertson makes it clear that this method of rationing must focus participation all the more tightly on career utility to the student, as defined either by a double-guess of employers' expectations or by the very dictate of some particular employer. He refrains from calling it rationing, perhaps because there is no central agency making the choice, perhaps because he is simply blind to the irony. Nonetheless, there is no apparent likelihood of unrestricted participation or extensive choice in this scheme. In fact, it must drastically limit educational opportunity for any individual student all the more rigorously by tying it to the demands not even of the economy in general, but to the economic interpretations of employers and their own specific projects. But besides, why *this* form of rationing of 'the development of human potential' *can* be afforded – in the sense of being socially acceptable – is not explicitly addressed in the article in question. The only justification one can infer is that this will optimize the earnings of more learners in the longer run.[2] It is morally worth trading the possible scope of one's human development for the chance of a better job.

Considered more narrowly as a scheme for the distribution of funds for tertiary education, this might be more equitable than the situation we have at present, of narrowly forced choices in conditions of excessive scarcity of resources. But it is by no means obvious that it would be more equitable than the social democratic response of increasing the availability of public funds. It is quite obvious that even if it enfranchised more people as 'learners', the cost would be an enormous restriction in their educational opportunities in comparison with the potential offered by public funding, which is relatively immune from the restricting game of double-guessing future business needs. (Notice how the very word 'learner' is subtly degraded here, no longer referring to someone who freely exercises an interest in knowing more, but rather to someone whose current occupation is to go through the routines of instrumental learning.)

If Robertson opposes increased public funding, it can only be because he wishes to change entirely the terms on which we value higher education in the first place. He does not see it as enriching the economy through dissemination of open-ended knowledge, critical or creative engagement with practical research or the unpredictable play of innovative skill – the payback in such cases is too uncertain for private investment to be efficient as social redistribution. And he certainly doesn't see it as the social reproduction of those values, that culture or those ethical commitments that make the economic future of society worth bothering with in the first place. He doesn't even seem to see it in terms of naked national survival in a globalized economy – who would entrust that, in the case of higher education, to the vagaries of the educational market choices of sixth-formers? For Robertson, tertiary education, including higher education, is an instrument of social engineering, the pursuit of a minor redistribution of wealth through a major impoverishment of expectations.[3] The antithesis of his goal is not the system of Oxbridge privilege, but the modest humanist idealism of the Open University.

We did not need to look at Robertson to know that funding schemes have moral presuppositions and moral implications. But the case of Robertson is useful to show that revised moral commitments can then entail shifts in educational aim and values, and that these can be covertly drastic. What one learns from looking at a proposal such as Robertson's is that the moral and political implications of a funding scheme can't be realistically assessed without looking closely at the educational (and thus economic) implications.

But there simply has not been the kind of serious considered debate about aims and values within higher education which is needed to address these implications. Dearing was far too superficial. So it is probably not for reasons like Robertson's that most leaders in higher education reject the social democratic strategy (as he himself laments, considering those sad Vice Chancellors who haven't seen his point (Robertson, 1996: 155)). On the other hand, in the political world considerations of educational values and implications are swept brusquely to one side as irrelevant to perceived need. Yet whether this is politically or economically wise in itself is something we very much doubt. The educational implications seem politically and economically negative, as we shall argue.

However, the world of the DfEE (Department for Education and Employment) and the CVCP (Committee of Vice-Chancellors and Principals) is a thoroughly hard-nosed place these days. Debate about fees has proceeded on the axiom that funding them wholly through general and progressive taxation just isn't going to happen. The debate is pragmatic at the highest levels, not moral. Typically, for instance, again we find Robertson baldly claiming that 'the state can no longer afford to fund lifelong learning wholly from general taxation; individuals and employers must be encouraged to contribute' (Robertson, 1996: 154–5). This is obviously intended to act as a kind of rhetorical 'stun gun', to frighten off such otherwise obvious responses as 'We have not yet had an enacted policy of lifelong learning, so there is no question of a new failure in our ability to fund it. Moreover, the new government's "war chest" for public expenditure before the election is historically enormous, whilst this remains an undertaxed country. There is anyway currently some economic case for raising taxation to choke off inflationary pressures. Besides, individuals and employers have always privately funded the purely vocational and non-university aspects of lifelong learning; so the only real question is why this should be extended to cover university education too'.

But these new arrangements nonetheless seem ineluctable, and we shall eventually consider why. Either way, however, there is pressing reason to examine their proposed justification. In particular, the proposals for tuition fees carry radically new implications for how we conceptualize and value higher education. These implications seem barely considered even by those who make the argument against them. Yet in the long run, the pressure to conform, if only unconsciously, to this new picture will in itself alter practice, if only imperceptibly. Over time, small changes will mount up to radical change.

In defence of charging tuition fees, a moral argument is proposed which says, in bare essentials, that higher education should be funded by those who benefit from it. This argument has two uses. On the one hand, it is invoked to justify the replacement of maintenance grants by means-tested loans, and we do not choose to quarrel with this. On the other, it is also used to justify demanding a means-related contribution to tuition fees. And in respect of tuition fees, it is imperative to ask: just who does benefit from higher education?

It appears to be the view of the Government, and contrary to the terms of current public debate, everybody. The two-thirds of younger people who will not attend university, and their families, will indeed benefit from higher education. For there is an interest that everyone has in living in a modern industrial state, which itself in turn requires a major input from higher education in order to thrive and develop. But the majority should not pay for higher education directly as they benefit from it only indirectly. Students, however, will benefit directly and so too will employers, both public and private. Therefore students, once they are graduates, should pay directly. (The obligations of employers are dodged, of course.) Those who do not benefit directly but only indirectly will nonetheless contribute to the university education of the minority through their taxes. (Here we are reconstructing the argument implicit in the direction of policy. It is not obvious that explicit statements of the argument are made in this form. Nonetheless, we believe that this is the clearest construction to put on the matter.)

In addition to this, the arrangements will have various elements of equity written in. A third of students from poorer backgrounds will pay nothing. A third will make only a partial contribution. Moreover, repayments will only be required once the graduate is working and earning more than a certain minimum (currently £10 000). Students of policy reassure us that the aim is to ensure that no one is disadvantaged and discouraged from pursuing higher education if they have the ability to do so. Moreover, this arrangement is thought to improve equity in a situation where the level of take-up varies vastly (and the gap widens) between the most- and least-favoured social classes.

The direct contribution of costs from graduates as a whole is to be 'only' about 25 per cent of the total of tuition fees, paid by loan. (This figure will vary, though, between individual students.) The situation with regard to maintenance is claimed to be unaffected in the immediate cost to students and their parents while they study. And it is claimed as an improvement, perhaps fairly, that front-loaded loans are to become back-loaded loans, related to achieved ability to pay rather than to initial circumstances.

The financial ins and outs and distributive details of the new funding proposals fall outside our realm of competence as philosophers of education. However, what does seem clear to us is that another dimension, important for the long-term development of higher education and for its role in our society, is being completely overlooked. As political realists (we trust), we might just 'bow to the inevitable' of loans for student fees if they really can be shown to be economically necessary. But we do insist, for reasons which follow, that if these arrangements are just plainly and simply practically imperative, then that fact should be

clearly recognized, publicly stated *and moreover regretted* as their rationale. What is indefensible is to inveigle the public into an ideological
commitment to a destructive view of the nature of higher education and
its justification, in order to defend not quite the indefensible but at best a
necessary evil. If students are indeed to clock up debts for their higher
education, let them at least be clear as to why they are doing so and, most
importantly of all, what they are doing it for – what they may take to be
the point of a university education.

It seems a truism beyond need of saying that university education has
not succeeded in any form at all unless students come out of it with a
better understanding of what they have studied than when they went
in. (Knowledge without understanding is worthless. If students are to be
valued for no more than the ability to tell employers 'facts' which they
need to know, then it has to be said that a good book, a library or a
browse on the Internet is cheaper.) But this does need saying because it
entails a less obvious but fundamentally important point. No one can
understand what they have studied unless they have also understood
the point of studying it. To see the point of an academic exercise is either
to see how it connects to other concerns, academic, moral, economic or
whatever (its extrinsic value); or to see some intrinsic value in it, its
'value in itself.' Neither of these aspects are external or luxury 'add-ons'
to any kind of academic study (not even the extrinsic), for they indicate
just how that study may be most fruitfully further developed, deep-
ened, extended, revised, reformed and so on. (Developing a dimension
or direction of research in a subject for no other reason than that it is possible to do so is the most trivial form of academicism. This is not the same
as 'curiosity-driven research'. The curious researcher typically has reasons for her curiosity, grounded in a sense of intrinsic value.) And to fail
to understand any subject, discourse, field, tradition or discipline in
such ways is in a very real sense to mistake it for something static, closed,
dogmatic, even arbitrary and other than it is; and thus to be incapable of
using one's knowledge at all fruitfully, either in application or in the further development of pure research. To fail to see the point of some study
is to fail to learn it in any worthwhile or usable way.

But no such understanding can be fully valid until a fairly advanced
stage of the study. One can't see 'the point' of work in a discipline or subject area unless one has a reasonably clear and adequately comprehensive view of what that discipline or subject actually is. This is a basic
point of logic. But it has practical implications: in particular, that one can,
because one must, tolerate a degree of unclarity in the motives of

students when they begin studying. If they had clear ideas why they were going into higher education from the beginning, that would either pre-empt at least some of students' own potential for enlightenment or have to be quickly abandoned. (The old Soviet expectation that students should go to university for precise reasons from which they do not swerve, is not one we should envy or admire at all but rather view as inherently incoherent.)

We are going to argue that in the light of the necessarily lengthy development of this understanding, higher education intrinsically entails a transformative effect on students that renders stakeholding arguments flatly inapplicable. Those who would like to resist going where this argument will lead might try to suggest that the points just made about understanding this may be true as far as they go, but that the practical implications for higher education are negligible. The beginning student, it might be suggested, already knows quite enough about the point of a subject for this not to need to be a significant issue in their further learning at university.

But this is just wildly implausible. In the case of school subjects continued at university, it suggests that there is (and need only be) straightforward continuity between the aims of, say, A-level English and physics and degree level English and physics – a view most academics (and indeed schoolteachers, not to say many theorists of either compulsory or post-compulsory education) would reject as preposterous – entailing as much distortion of the school curriculum as degradation of degree work. (The Moser Report was just one of many statements objecting to the tying of the sixth form curriculum to the aims of university study. Even where they may be expected to go on to university, the education of the young has other important aims, even in the purely academic sphere. The young deserve a broader picture of the worlds of learning and culture, not to mention moral, aesthetic and political development.) Secondly, as to non-school subjects, it suggests that one needs no better understanding of their point – for life – than that which an interested sixth-former might pick up in the course of some casual reading about, say, philosophy, political science, psychology or law.

Third, and alarmingly, it would put a question mark against the very legitimacy of academics in any discipline or subject area rethinking the point and purpose of their work to any significant degree (as has happened in so many over the past three decades). It would entail a kind of Academic Settlement precluding radical reconceptualizations. Thus, to resist the argument that university education involves deep consideration and reconsideration of the point and purpose of one's study is to propose a picture of it inimical to academic freedom in the pursuit of knowledge.

Views of higher education such as these would present it as essentially value-free or non-contestable. They are theoretical objections, not yet much in evidence but useful to keep at bay, since the exercise of thinking through the possible, if not actual, arguments redirects attention more precisely to the area of real contestation. For any view of higher education effectively imposed on students which obscures or confuses their understanding of the point of what they are doing cannot but, in effect, undermine that very pursuit of understanding which is the most elementary aim of higher education. But the form of the argument over funding is in danger of causing precisely such confusion and unclarity insofar as it is proposed as the new political common sense for intending and future students.

The current argument seems to be in effect a version of that commitment to stakeholding which many of us on the centre-left had quite recently seen as their best hope from a Labour government. Yet the conspicuous fact is that stakeholding, originally and paradigmatically an ethic for private and public enterprise, has been quietly forgotten in almost every field except that of higher education. Nonetheless, it is to be pressed opportunistically into service in the very context which, we will argue, is the least appropriate for its use. Let us say immediately that in arguing against a stakeholder view of higher education, we are not arguing against democratization in higher education, either in terms of internal governance or in terms of widening access – or indeed in the relation of higher education to the State. Rather, we argue against an inappropriately economistic view of education that conceives it as a commodity available in a market, and universities as market providers with stakeholders. (Nor, of course, are we arguing against stakeholding in relation to organizations that actually are part of a market.)

We begin to see that stakeholding is inappropriate once we take seriously the transformative effect of higher education. To come to understand the point of an area of study is to be oneself transformed to some degree as a person, because to come to see the value in the study is to come to value it oneself. This is not wholly obvious. It might seem that one could in principle understand why the practitioners within an academic field see it as valuable without seeing it that way oneself, without personal commitment to the same values. Indeed patently this is the attitude of some students to work they do not value or enjoy. It is a 'view from the outside'. But seeing or not seeing the supposed value as genuine is not a matter of giving or withholding approbation, like some detached political gesture. As we argued above, it is a matter of seeing or not seeing how the study can be fruitfully developed in various ways. To know how it might be developed, either in itself or in its external relations to other concerns or practices, is both to understand and to see its value. To fail to see this is not to value, but not to understand either. It is no accident that students who fail to commit to the values of their chosen study seem, anecdotally, to be poor students. In a very real and live sense, they have 'failed to understand'.

So to come to understand what one studies at university is to change one's values and commitments. It is, in effect, to be transformed as a person – to have new values which may entail revised views as to one's appropriate project in life and what may count as a problem worth dealing with or an issue to be ignored. (If we did not, until the advent of the Open University, seriously believe university to be a place for adult students, that surely reflected a deep lack of faith in the potential of grown adults for any further personal transformation at all – a view we nowadays find virtually scandalous.)

But to conceive oneself as a stakeholder in an enterprise is precisely to see oneself as *not* transformed by that enterprise. The whole point of the stakeholder conception is that those engaged in the enterprise under consideration are not described exhaustively by their life in relation to that enterprise. If shareholders have a stake in a firm, it's because their shares are an element in their personal wealth that is properly a private concern of their own, not acceptably subject to the requirements of some firm they happen to invest in. Similarly, if the workers in a firm are stakeholders, it is precisely because their work impinges not only on their wealth but also on their legitimate interests as, for instance, parents, spouses, perhaps carers, leading legitimate lives of their own. To be defined as a stakeholder is precisely to be defined as someone who has the right to resist any transformation by the enterprise without having some say in that transformation, because one has other legitimate concerns of one's own. (This is not to say that work should never be allowed a transformative influence – the best work always does – but rather to say that this should be a matter of the autonomous involvement of the stakeholder herself. It is up to the individual nurse, for instance, to control the ways and the degree to which she defines herself by nursing.)

Can higher education not be conceived this way? Why can't the student be thought of as someone who, though she might be partially transformed by successful study, nonetheless retains some core identity that remains essentially untouched by education and external to it, and can be conceived as the holder of some stake in the process? It is part of the logic of values that this is not possible. Values cannot be held apart from each other. Intrinsically they form hierarchies of justification and levels of priority amongst themselves. Often there are conflicts between values or issues of balance which need resolution by the person whose values they are. In so resolving them, she redefines herself completely, if not necessarily radically. The values and commitments a graduate comes to hold through academic study cannot be isolated from some non-academic core self that may be conceived as the stakeholder in her education. Those values necessarily become part of any core self and modify it, perhaps a little, perhaps drastically yet nonetheless unavoidably.

(The case just imagined of the nurse who decides for herself how much she is defined by nursing is interesting in this connection. For she might be thought the very model of a graduate who stands in an external relation to her studies, and thus arguably a stakeholder in it. But this isn't so. For in relation to her training as a nurse, indeed she cannot properly withdraw some core self from the exercise – though see below for some counter-productive ways of trying to do so. In seeing the point and value of nursing, she has to adjust these perceptions to her other values, perhaps religious or political or more general values of caring. On the other hand, she may nonetheless still conceive herself externally to a particular hospital as a stakeholder, which in turn may modify her self-definition as a nurse. This is only too often the case today when best nursing practice runs up against incompatible management demands in the health sector. Thus the nurse can maintain at the same time an internal relation to her training, with no core self withheld; and an external, stakeholding relation to her hospital, in which she would want, if possible, autonomy in the service of a core self independent of the institution.)

The same kinds of consideration highlight the absurdity of the fashionable notion in policy debate that students in post-compulsory education should be thought of as investing in their own human capital (itself used as an argument in favour of fees for tuition). David Robertson (1996), as a leading voice in the debate over lifelong learning, quotes Glennerster with approval: 'The aim of public policy is [sic] to ensure that individuals invest optimally in their own human capital and have the resources to do so'.[4]

This is doubly ridiculous where the learning addresses any developed academic discipline, discourse or field. First, to invest in anything is an instrumental activity. One invests as a means to some further goal, itself accepted therein as settled. But the whole point about this kind of study is, as we have argued, that one's view of the purpose of the study is something that necessarily changes. Indeed, we might add that the better the understanding a graduate has achieved, the greater the possibility that her view of the purpose of the study will continue to develop and change even after she has graduated, whether or not she continues in further study. This kind of 'investment' might be thought to be, at best, investment in a Magical Mystery Tour; at worst, investment in a pig in a poke. It is not genuine investment at all – thank goodness.

Conversely, to think of one's studies as something in which it makes sense to 'invest' is to think of them as having some predeterminable 'pay-off', such that the success of the study, indeed of the course itself, may properly be judged by its efficacy in securing this pay-off. But to think this is to set limits in advance on what one will bother to learn or may even be able to understand in one's study. We have surely all taught the instrumentalist student who doesn't understand some idea, some caveat, some alien train of thought, because it fails to speak to her own settled and unswerving aims. (In the same spirit, instrumentalist educationists sometimes pretend to view educational theory as incomprehensible.) It is, as most academics know from sour experience, for the student to commit herself to incomprehension from the beginning. To 'invest' in understanding is to foreclose upon it.

(Anecdotally and for illustration, another author of this book tells of a student who objected that his course had not been effectively reduced to a series of consumable bullet-points. The subject was the philosophy of social science – arguably *inter alia* a critique of bullet-points.)

Notice that this is not an argument against study for vocational purposes. The problem is not the student who studies engineering to become an engineer. The problem is the student whose conception of engineering is settled before she begins the course and who is inured to reconsideration of the nature or point of the enterprise. Such a student is destined to become a social liability – a bad engineer.

If the idea of investing in oneself is harmful here, so too is the more basic idea of the development of one's own human capital; not because transformation is not wanted from education but on the contrary, because this way of conceiving things is inimical to such transformation. If 'human capital' is a metaphor, consider first its primary use. It does make

19

some kind of sense to speak of the management of a firm developing the firm's human capital. Just as management properly looks to add to, upgrade or replace its physical plant, so too it may wish to do much the same with its workforce. Wise managers, of course, will avoid thinking of their staff as nothing other than animate factors of production. Nonetheless, the metaphor of human capital has some defensible meaning here. But this directs our attention to another aspect of the instrumentalism encoded in the idea of investing in human capital. It makes sense only where the investors are one set of people, the 'human capital' another – where the one is external to the other. This is so even in the most democratic of organizations. However well the workforce may be consulted and involved in their 'development', the ultimate purposes are those of the firm, not of its workers as individuals or groups. Even in those enlightened enterprises which encourage all manner of personal development in their staff, not immediately or obviously geared to the internal processes of the organization, the ultimate rationale remains that of running a successful firm.

There is nothing scandalous in this, of course. It is rather the inevitable externality between the human capital and its 'developers' that matters. Because as we have seen, given the logic and nature of values and understanding, no such externality is possible between 'one's own human capital' and oneself. For a student to think of her own knowledge and understanding as intellectual capital is once again for her to alienate her own intellectual resources from some core self: a core which redirects those resources according to values and understanding untouched by what she has learnt and understood in the course of her own study – a core which remains untransformed.

Is such a person possible? Psychology shows us that many peculiar ways of being are possible, not least ways of splitting the personality; but it also shows us their cost. In this case, the cost of alienating one's academic understanding from one's self – as writers such as Robertson clearly think, alienated from one's social and civic self – is a severe degradation in understanding of one's studies and thus in academic achievement. This splitting does not obviate the problem of organizing one's values into hierarchies and priorities or resolving conflicts between them. But it entails a particular kind of solution: which is to decide *a priori* that academic values and understanding have the lowest priority in one's view of life and no explanatory or ordering force for one's stance towards life (and, thus, towards society and the economy). But what is truly objectionable here is not so much the lowly position of academic values and understanding, not some imagined affront to cultural elitism, but the necessary incomprehension of academic values which follows from any decision to put them in such a place *a priori*. To make the decision *a priori* is to make it without reference to the understanding academic study affords. It is thus, almost inevitably, to enact a systematic misunderstanding of one's studies.

As we have seen, this must entail an academic cost in terms of learning. Just as 'investment' in understanding forecloses upon it, so too one can only stunt one's intellectual growth by conceiving it as one's human capital, in some sense alienated from a core self which takes all the serious decisions in one's life, uncompromised by academic values and understanding. Not least, it is a hidden cost to those who are supposed to benefit from this marketised and commodifying view of higher education, namely employers. If potential students are successfully encouraged to see themselves as 'investing in their own human capital', it is the quality of graduates that will suffer and their value to the economy which will decline.

It won't do, at this point, for instrumentalists and desperate cash-strapped educational managers to lose patience and say, 'This is a fuss about nothing, an aesthetic objection to a robust form of words. All we really mean by "investing in one's own human capital" is paying for one's own education – and even then only in part'. The justification offered for this, to recap, is a view of the student as a stakeholder in education, and not by any means the only one. It is a view of higher education as having instrumentalist purposes, if not exclusively then nonetheless increasingly so and primarily. But it is precisely the view of the student as a stakeholder which is educationally regressive; and our examination of the metaphor of investing in one's own human capital is a heuristic for heightening our sense of the 'learning cost' of this instrumentalism. But if these arguments hold, they force on us a very practical and disturbing political possibility: that even if government (meaning in fact the state) and employers have a stake in education, students themselves can't properly be thought of that way.

This possibility highlights a further conceptual oddity of the current argument. For of course, a stake is only one particular kind of interest. One may have an interest in some institution or activity or state of affairs, without necessarily having either a stake in it, as an involved party whose other and differing interests are relevant to balance against the interests of the other stakeholders, or an investment on which some return might be due. If students do not have a *stake* in their higher education as such, they certainly have the most intimate of interests in it, by being, for the dura-tion, wholly immersed in it (and not just partially, like a stakeholder). Even if the state and employers have stakes, students nonetheless have important interests too.

What does this difference between stakes, investments and other kinds of interest come to, though, in practical terms? To have an investment is to have a right to a very limited kind of return, whose nature can be pre-specified and whose size is objectively calculable. To have a stake is to have a right to representation and to vote in decision making which may affect one's other interests. But to have an interest in the more familiar moral sense is not necessarily to have a voice in decision making – though, contingently, representation seems essential in this case too. More importantly, it is legitimately to require not simply that one's inter-ests may be balanced against others in compromises, but that one's inter-ests are intrinsic to the decision to be made. If the decision-making process does not from the start acknowledge one's interests as relevant criteria for the decision (if obviously not the only criteria), then it is not merely politically unacceptable, it is simply not appropriate or relevant. To say that students have an interest that is not a stake in higher educa-tion is not at all to alienate their interests from decision making, but on the contrary to put them back at its very heart, from which the stakeholding metaphor subtly distances them.

Yet even if this is so, it might still be argued that the state and employers have interests, which may even be stakes. As stakes, they would amount to some kind of external veto or compulsion on educational arrange-ments. For whatever intrinsic interest students (and academics also) may have in the process, that does not legitimate its impairment of legiti-mate external interests. But the students' interest then will not be impor-tant enough to 'trump' actual stakes that are held by employers and the state. So, does the student turn out to be nothing but a factor in the sys-tem, whose interests come last? The only way to dodge this disturbing alternative is to question whether government and business are best conceived as stakeholders either.

There are in fact two questions we may ask at this point. One would be the ethical question of whether state and business should be thought of as having stakes. Another, more political and at this point more perti-nent, would be whether this possibility is in fact taken seriously in the current proposals. (This too is a philosophical question, concerning pre-suppositions and implications of those proposals.) We can deliver a fairly confident 'No' to the question of the business interest. (For brevity, we will pass over the state's interest.)

There are two ways we might think of business as having such a stake. First, it might be that specific businesses have specific stakes in the participation of particular students in particular courses. This is indeed proposed as a possible (and occasionally already actual) arrangement with respect to further and continuing education of various sorts. But for higher education, this kind of role is, and seems likely to remain, at most marginal. If business has a stake here, it must surely be business as a whole that is thought of as having a general stake in higher education as a whole. But is this consonant with the proposed arrangements?

However ill-advised it is to think of students as having a stake in higher education, it is only as a stake in their own education that it is even credible, not as a stake in the system as a whole. The benefits accruing to them from a live higher education sector, other than the purely personal, are cultural and economic benefits shared by every citizen, for which everyone might reasonably pay through their taxes. So at best one might say that, even if business and students are both stakeholders, they are not stakeholders in the same things. If business has a stake in higher education as a whole, students might at most be misconceived as stakeholders in their own personal higher education. This itself is the ground of a potential clash of interests that no reference to stakeholding could possibly resolve.

But even if this were acknowledged to be the situation, business is not actually funding its own stake. The government somewhat surreptitiously tips the funding scales towards science and technology courses, presumably because these are thought more useful economically. One way in which it does so is by weighting them favourably when allocating teaching funds. But it also proposes to make students subsidize this imbalance. The proposed tuition fees will be flat-rate. But the costs of teaching vary enormously between social science and humanities courses on the one hand, and science and technology on the other. So one group of students are to subsidize another, paying a larger proportion of their fees. But this can't be justified whether we conceive their 'stake' to be either purely personal or that of the citizen at large. If some differential subsidy were nonetheless justified, and it almost certainly is, it would necessarily fall to business to foot a large slice of the bill, for it is their stake, if they truly have one, which dictates the imbalance of government funds. Further, they would almost certainly need to subsidize students who wish to follow these more expensive courses, or else accept that their manpower could only be drawn from the small pool of those rich enough to pay the extra to do so.[5]

Tuition fees, then, are ultimately justified, inasfar as they are justified at all, as nothing more than a form of surrogate taxation which in turn will fund a covert subsidy to business, substituting for what might be thought the contribution they owe, given their 'stake'. The only excuse for such fees is that the government might 'get away' with a quasi-tax on the overt beneficiaries of higher education. There is no rationale for them in terms of social justice or personal advantage. So the question then becomes: why do we need to resort to this underhand form of taxation at all? Just what is wrong, after all, with the social democratic response, that higher education must be paid for (as must so much else) from rises in general taxation on the country at large? The answer, we suggest, may have to do with globalization.

In his recent book, *False Dawn: The Delusions of Global Capitalism*, John Gray argues that

> Global capital markets... make social democracy unviable. By social democracy mean the combination of deficit-financed full employment, a comprehensive welfare state and egalitarian tax policies... [The social democratic regime of Britain until the late 1970s] presupposed a closed economy. Capital movements were limited by fixed or semi-fixed exchange rates... it is only in a closed economy that egalitarian principles can be enforced. In open economies they will be rendered unworkable by the freedom of capital – including 'human capital' – to migrate. (Gray, 1998: 88–9)

and he adds,

> The classic solution to the problems of financing the provision of public goods is mutually agreed coercion.... This classic solution breaks down when taxation is not enforceable on mobile capital and corporations. If sources of revenue – capital, enterprises and people – are free to migrate to low-tax regimes, mutually agreed coercion does not work as a means for paying for public goods. The kinds and level of taxation levied in order to pay for public goods in any state cannot significantly exceed those found in states that are otherwise comparable. (Gray, 1998: 89)

His point has a double interest for us. First, there is a case for governments to restrain social spending as tightly as they can, for fear of scaring off international capital. Taxes must be kept as low as possible, for reasons which have little to do with the monetarist policies of the past. And secondly, part of the reason for this is precisely that major business interests *just don't* have any 'stake' in particular countries at all. The multinationals may have a generalized interest in education. But they do not have a specific stake in higher education in the UK rather than, say, Ireland or Taiwan.

Is this the understanding that informs Treasury policy? It is hard to prove, but also hard to doubt it. It seems clearly to inform our political leaders. 'In the age of the global economy, only the open, nimble and lightly regulated will thrive', said William Hague in his Fontainebleau speech of May, 1998. And a *Guardian* leader added ruefully the next day, 'oddly enough, Mr. Blair says similar things, albeit in France, and also extols free trade'.[6]

If multinationals have no stake in British higher education, the notional stake of small and medium enterprises (SMEs) is surely rather a stake in further and continuing education. Their interest in research is necessarily met less directly (preferably in concert with each other and on co-operative terms with universities rather than as stakeholders[7]). This leaves only those large firms that are not yet multinational who are even candidates for stakeholder status. But this is far too small a subset of industry to justify a reconceptualization of higher education that would be either principled or economically worthwhile.

If students themselves are not well conceived as stakeholders, then to call the state a stakeholder, in this minimal context, is no more than the platitude that government investment in education has to be balanced against other demands. Ultimately, there are no stakeholders in higher education – it just isn't that kind of enterprise.

So what kind of enterprise is it? In the panic of globalization, it seems to have been forgotten that higher education is an inherently critical business, and that critique is not some cultural indulgence but a practical necessity. A remarkable and worrying characteristic of the Dearing Report is how much it takes for granted which is properly (and often actually) a matter of serious academic debate. Globalization, and how to react to it is itself such an issue. If we are really serious about it, then we should be slower to take it for granted that, like Blair and Hague, we 'know' what will and won't prosper in this future (which, after all, is meant to extend just a bit further than the next election or two).

In particular, as we note elsewhere in this book, some very glib assumptions are currently being made about the supposed need for flexibility in the workforce. But there is room for serious doubt as to whether the 'flexibility' of mere biddability will be enough – drop what you were doing before, chaps, and try something else. It is being forgotten that higher education, as understood for the last half century, is itself concerned with a real flexibility within disciplines and vocations, far deeper and further-reaching than any offered at the Dearing smorgasbord. A good statistician, biochemist or lawyer is flexible *as* a mathematician, biochemist, lawyer and so on. She can move forward to new developments on her own field whilst pausing to reassess the nature of what she does. It is she who is in that vanguard of modernity by which the growth economy has so far been pulled along. And, as a learner, she does not foreclose on her possibilities. She takes her subject seriously in its own right, following it where she had not thought to go.

If we are to be indeed an open economy, we must have an open ideology of higher education too. The deceptive stakeholder conception promises to foreclose on the very modernity we need. A dumbed-down student body will offer nothing to the project of our economic survival. As a harbinger of this closure, charging for tuition fees must be seen as a very dangerous ideological signal indeed.

Notes

1. The details of funding that follow have been checked against the article by Baroness Blackstone (Minister for Higher Education), 'Ability to pay tops the bill' (Blackstone, 1997b).
2. Robertson's other arguments are even flimsier. The second is that government expenditure 'tends to favour already privileged social groups'. Since the privilege is identified in terms of educational achievement, a view of education as investment (such as Robertson's) might dictate the very same policy. The third is that government funding 'removes incentives for individuals and employers to make their own investments in lifelong learning' – as if the time and effort of study were not investments already and the financial investment something valuable in its own right.
3. It was the Robertsons of working-class life whom Ernest Bevin chided for 'the poverty of their expectations'.
4. Robertson (1996) is quoting Glennerster (1991).
5. Our thanks to Professor Ruth Jonathan for drawing our attention to these anomalies.
6. This refers to Blair's speech to the French National Assembly, March 1998, reported in *The Guardian*, 21 May 1998.
7. This is discussed further in Chapter 6. See also Blake (1998).

2

What We Teach and What Students Learn

The argument of this chapter is that the university curriculum has changed in such a way that procedural values have triumphed over content. The promotion of procedural values has coincided with, and has partially been justified by, the belief that in a rapidly changing world it is above all transferable skills and the ability to go on learning that are needed. There is an obvious plausibility to this view. It seems moreover that this justification rests largely on notions of the return to society that graduates can make and, by implication, on assumptions about the common good. Contrary to this, however, we shall argue that the emphasis on the procedural undermines and constitutes a threat to the public benefit that should be derived from higher education. To argue this we shall need to show what that public benefit consists of.

CHANGE AND DIVERSITY

One problem with broaching questions of the university curriculum is diversity. There is a historical impetus to the university that has, in the past, justified a certain introspection about its essence. In the early 1990s Jaroslav Pelikan revisited Newman's classic text, *The Idea of a University*, exploring the terms and the trajectory of his argument for their contemporary significance. Very recently influential figures such as Stewart Sutherland and Ronald Barnett have argued that the question, 'What is a university?' needs to be asked again, and that it is to philosophers especially that we might turn for answers. It is true that there continues to be a potency to the question, though this now derives in part from a source very alien to Newman and to other leading figures in the development of the university over the past two centuries – the discourse of presentation and accountability. There is a dearth of such visionary characterizations now, and though Dearing may style itself 'a vision for higher education over the next 20 years' (para. 4), formulations of the essence of the university now are likely to be evident more in smaller scale stipulations of curriculum intention, in the apparatus of quality control, and more grandly perhaps in mission statements.

It needs to be asked first, however, how far it can be appropriate to speak of the idea of *the* university – how far this is appropriate now and, for that matter, how far it has been in the past. For it needs to be recognized that key texts in the history of the idea of the university, such as Newman's, have generally been those that outlined a vision rather than those that described current practice, and hence these do not offer a full picture of what was going on at the time. No doubt there is more diversity now than there was but the dangers of oversimplifying the past are not to be underestimated.

But whatever the variations in universities have been in the past it is clear that the diversity we now see is of a different order, the ending of the binary divide and the expansion of participation being the most obvious reasons for this. With the change in status of polytechnics and some colleges of higher education, the wider range of courses offered by these institutions became by fiat university courses. In certain respects this was no more than to recognize in the nomenclature the parity that, to the extent that these institutions offered degree courses, had for some time obtained. Whatever suspicions some may have harboured about the relative merits of these degrees, they were every bit as much BAs and BScs as university courses. If these degrees had once been the exclusive province of the university, this had for a long time ceased to be the case.

The influence of increased access and of its attendant principles on the curriculum has been more complex. The extension of participation is underpinned by two major principles. The first is that the country needs a more highly educated population especially so that its economic competitiveness can be enhanced. Globalization, it is held, makes this all the more imperative. This is predominantly a pragmatic principle then, however much those wedded to market economics may wish to see in it a fitting response to the natural order of things. The second principle concerns equality, particularly the extension of opportunity. Access programmes targeted at mature students whose earlier schooling has not given them the qualifications needed for university or at other disadvantaged groups, as well as those aimed at school leavers who have not, for reasons of disadvantage, made the grade, are largely compensatory in kind: they make up for deficiencies in the ability of the educational system to provide adequately for these people at earlier stages. Both principles – the need for a better educated population and the extension of opportunity – are advanced in the name of democracy. The economic prosperity that a more highly educated workforce will bring is a major contributor to the common good and to enabling people to share in the goods that society offers. Stakeholder conceptions of society presuppose the possibility of this kind of involvement. The principle of equality emphasizes another aspect of democracy, however. This is the empowerment of individuals. We need to examine the effects of these principles in order to see how they have affected the curriculum.

One effect of the emphasis on economic competitiveness has been an equalization of the status of subjects such that vocational courses have gained a kind of parity of esteem. Indeed this may be an understatement in that in certain respects and in some quarters subjects such as business studies and accountancy have acquired a kind of kudos derived from their supposed relevance to the 'real world' and from their potential as pathways to lucrative careers – in contrast especially to 'soft' subjects in the humanities. This shift in attitudes has been desirable to the extent that it has counterbalanced an earlier snobbery that downgraded technological activities in favour of the academic, one that existed in a slightly different form, where the arts were opposed to the sciences, in C P Snow's 'two cultures'. But one outcome of this equalization of esteem, superficial though this may have been, has been a caution about criticizing subjects in terms of their substance. Quite simply this diversification has undermined the criteria that were tacitly assumed for judging the appropriateness of a subject's place on the university curriculum. What amounts to a shying away from substantive judgements has institutionalized a kind of non-judgmentality that is familiar enough today. There is a spirit of democratization that says not only that there should be an equality of subjects but that these should be equally available through such curriculum design techniques as modularization. The ending of the binary divide has tended to cause universities to try to be all things to all students. Against this aspiration the cutting of funds has forced them to curtail their activities in certain respects, and the competitive pressures of the market, with the new accentuation that students' responsibility for their own fees has created, has encouraged them to emphasize whatever distinctiveness they have in order to secure their own market niche. A video promoting the university will be at pains to highlight what is, say, 'the Bristol experience', in this case generating perhaps a kind of mystique attaching to tradition and style, and relying in part on the afterglow of images from an earlier era. A newer university may emphasize its multicultural feel, its practical approach, and the night life in the town. The point is that these promotions emphasize *how* things are done at particular universities, more or less regardless of the course a student enrols for – and, holiday brochure style, it is usually emphasized that there is something for everyone. Given the fact that most students go away from home to study, it is not surprising that such an emphasis is made and that the ambience of a place, its customs and traditions, its parodies of initiation rites perhaps, should come to be highlighted. Moreover there is no shortage of publications now that make comparisons between universities – *Which?* report fashion – on the basis not so much of course content but of matters such as these.

The way that attention has been deflected from the *substance* of courses here is matched by a similar deflection arising from the principle of equality of opportunity directed towards the empowerment of the individual. Empowerment may be understood, we would like to think, to incorporate a robust conception of citizenship where people take on the role of contributing to the development and shaping of their society in ways that are in part expressive of themselves but through which they in some sense *find* themselves. More likely, however, it is a different aspect, the freedom to choose, that will be foregrounded, and this will be interpreted in terms of curriculum choices. Those who have promoted access have shown a sensitivity to differences between students, a kind of student-centredness emphasizing the importance of student choice. Indeed, if the recommendations of the Fryer Report (here glossed in a *THES* pull-out) are followed in universities, the policy will be to move the emphasis away from the institution and on to the learners themselves:

> The focus of policy and practice should be learners themselves and the quality and range of learning opportunities made available to them. This would shift attention away from structures and institutions, which should be regarded as more or less efficient mechanisms for the delivery of high-quality learning in their given spheres. The support offered to learners should enable them increasingly to assume ownership of their own learning as they progress through life. The needs and voices of the learners should be given sufficient opportunities to be expressed, heard and responded to and organisations' success in this should be subject to review... All funders and providers should review the nature and relevance of programmes of study, learning outcomes and the qualifications offered to learners and would-be

learners. Providers have to be stimulated to offer what individuals, employers[,] community groups and others want, not merely what the provider has current capacity to deliver, or what presents fewest difficulties... [Managers] need to understand the needs of learners, through conducting systematic enquiry and analysis, and design programmes of study accordingly. (Fryer, 1997)

Increasingly then students' preferences will come to shape the curriculum. The priority will be, so it seems, the setting up of flexible curriculum systems that, for all their rules of combination and progression, enable students to determine their own pathways through that curriculum. The presumption will be, on the part of students and possibly staff too, that the appropriateness of a course is to be settled by reference to the students' preferences and inclinations, on the basis of pre-existing desires, albeit desires modified and developed by previous study, rather than on demands that the subject, the discipline, might make of them. The democratization of institutions thus dovetails with this democratized conception of students as autonomous choosers with the right (within limits) to determine their own individual learning pathways. If in the past the way a curriculum was devised has been the preserve of academics in the department concerned, if this has remained relatively arcane from the point of view of students ('That sounds interesting in Term Three. I wonder what it is'), the emphasis now is on a transparency that seems increasingly necessary if students are to select the course. Dearing is at pains to stress this: lifelong learning points to the need for higher education to 'be explicit about what it is providing through learning programmes and their expected outcomes, so that students and employers have a better understanding of their purposes and benefits' (1.18). And how entirely reasonable and commonsensical this can seem to be. That students pay for their courses themselves seems to set the seal *ex post facto* on the idea that they are after all customers of the system.

PROCEDURAL VALUES

Given the kind of vacuum regarding the criteria for content that is created by these changes it is not surprising that various rival factors have come to fill the space. The importance now attached to transferable skills, to the use of information technology, to the development of enterprise skills testifies to a concern with procedure and not content. It appears to finesse questions of content and to make more plausible the non-judgmental approach that is so widely approved.

The closing of the binary divide and the proliferation of university courses have provoked a certain lack of confidence both for the public and for universities themselves. Of course, there has been a rush to defend standards, which first and foremost for those running universities tends to mean simply reiterating the claim that standards are being maintained. The difficulty of believing that there is parity between courses has been a major stimulus behind the move towards systems of quality control, especially in the face of this new diversity. The Committee of Vice-Chancellors and Principals puts its weight behind these practices, arguing that the new framework of qualifications needs quality assurance systems that are robust, are cost-effective, and deliver proper public accountability (CVCP, 1998, para. 4). Yet the new jargon this generates – of learning outcomes, performance, and effectiveness – is asserted all the more volubly as anxiety over standards mounts.

It would be naïve to suppose that this current lack of confidence is the sole motivation behind this as such managerial practices are too deeply ingrained in the contemporary world to be properly understood as rational *ad hoc* responses to current problems in this respect. It would be closer to the truth to say that these practices partly determine what is to count as a problem. This is not to invoke any conspiracy theory but to acknowledge the way such systems have fostered our propensity to police ourselves: they are part of a more pervasive culture of surveillance.

In the current furore over *quality* and *standards* in education it is no surprise that these terms figure prominently in policy documents and debates on higher education. In March 1998 The Quality Assurance Agency (QAA) published its third issue of *Higher Quality*, a consultation issue seeking responses to the QAA's agenda for quality, based on the Dearing proposals. It is immediately apparent that this document conceives university education in service terms and the vocabulary of stakeholders is very much in evidence. Thus, in his prefatory remarks, Chief Executive John Randall explains that the QAA seeks to develop a system for assuring quality and standards that:

- is efficient, economical and reduces the burden of external scrutiny of institutions;
- satisfies the information needs of a wide range of stakeholders;
- enables funding bodies to satisfy themselves that value is being obtained for the public funds they distribute;

- enhances quality through continuous improvement;
- promotes public confidence in United Kingdom higher education.

Up to a point these aims are laudable enough. Anyone who argues that higher education today should disregard the interests of such stakeholders as the students themselves and employers will have an uphill struggle and rightly so. Given the huge public investment in higher education some measure of accountability is undoubtedly desirable. And how could anyone sensibly oppose the aims of continuous improvement and promoting public confidence? If some of these aims seem so vague as to be anodyne, this cannot be said of the desire to reduce the burden of external scrutiny of institutions; indeed in this aim the QAA seems to be responding to precisely that kind of issue that might most exercise those in universities. In so doing it is responding in a way that appears to be strongly supported by the CVCP (1998: paras 1, 9, 15). But there is a difficulty that it will be worth pursuing, for this will demonstrate how the problems of Dearing can derive even from its most benign aspects.

The concern to restrict the imposition of external scrutiny is manifested in the commitment expressed by Dearing to the system, widely supported by university staff, of external examiners. Dearing quite rightly identifies problems with existing practice arising especially as a result of the expansion of higher education and the proliferation of courses. The familiarity with existing practice in a subject that may have been possible for university examiners in the past, the informal contacts and networks that in many ways constituted the academic community, have become fragmented with the tensions and diversity of the new scale of provision. Where they are sustained, they are often riven with rival paradigms. Different 'cultures' have found themselves using the same course labels though perhaps without any common understanding of what their programmes should be about, still less of the criteria for successful learning. In the face of this Dearing proposes 'the establishment of formal groupings of academics to identify expectations for awards and achievements at the threshold and highest end of the spectrum for different types of programme' (para. 10.91). What is envisaged is a managed system involving the creation of a UK-wide pool of recognized academic staff from which all universities and other degree-awarding institutions must select external examiners. A small panel, managed by the QAA, would approve the inclusion of any individual on the nationally recognized list. As *Higher Quality* has it, the proposals would:

- give external examiners an explicit role in public assurance of quality and standards;
- create a national framework within which external examiners will operate;
- require external examiners to be registered and competent;
- create mechanisms which enable institutions to compare their academic standards in a more systematic and informed way.

The development of commonly accepted criteria for effective performance is held to be necessary for judging competence and the QAA has commissioned work to enable occupational standards and performance criteria for external examiners to be developed for consultation. While the QAA does not wish to interfere with the reporting of examiners to institutions this will be supplemented by an extended function whereby institutions will nominate experienced examiners to report to the QAA. The nature of the competence needed by these external examiners, as envisaged by the QAA, is worth considering:

> They will need to be well versed in the various methods used for assessment of student performance, to be familiar with the tasks of verifying and calibrating standards and to possess a clear understanding of their role. The QAA has a responsibility to deal with these latter areas and must ensure that appropriate standards of technical competence are developed. (QAA, 1998: 16)

There is an air of rigour here which masks the fact that it is far from clear what these competencies amount to or even mean. Of the number of assumptions embedded here, let us consider two. First, there is the question of the nature of the technical competence that the examiners will require. This would seem to amount to a familiarity with the methodology of assessment, where this is understood in terms independent from particular subjects: thus they should be familiar with different modes of assessment, with the different forms that coursework can take, with the pros and cons of oral examination, with the possibilities of computer aided testing, and so on. There is no doubt that everyone other than the corrupt wants a basic kind of efficiency from examiners – things must after all be done to a certain schedule – and there is no doubt that no one wants examiners who are incompetent in this or other respects. But the word permits a kind of sleight of hand, a self-deception perhaps, which Dearing and *Higher Quality* do not seem to avoid. For surely the competence that is wanted above all else is a competence in the subject being examined. Without this any amount of expertise in assessment methodology will be of little use. Indeed, it may be worse than useless in that it may surreptitiously cause the work to be driven by the nostrums of that methodology with its substitute rigour to the neglect of the requirements and the dynamics, indeed the true rigour, of the subject itself. The external examiner must above all be someone who is *au fait* with those requirements and dynamics. The best examiners are subject experts. And it will not do to say in response that, of course, subject expertise is expected, for it remains the case that the emphasis is on a new type of expertise – a generalized skill of examining – that, on the one hand, deflects attention from what is most central and, on the other, is likely to impose unduly on elements in teaching and learning previously determined more exclusively by the demands of the subject matter of the course. This then is the second matter of concern: that the demands of a subject are more or less eclipsed from these documents. The subject is understood in procedural terms to the neglect of subject matter.

We referred to the intention to maintain and support the system of external examining as benign but indicated that it harboured problems. Ultimately this support of the system involves an increased internal scrutiny. With the extension of reporting functions for external examiners and the requirements of registration, it is difficult to maintain the favourable impression that the recommendation encourages, notwithstanding the fact that the alternatives could have been far worse. For the desire to preserve the autonomy of institutions and academic departments occasions an extension of quality control.

Of course, there are strong arguments in favour of endeavouring to develop common standards within a subject. It is on the face of it quite unjust if the student who receives a 2:1 in History at Liverpool has had a much tougher time – has worked much harder, has studied more, has engaged in more difficult reading and assignments... (and there is no exhaustive list here) – than the person who receives the same grade for the same subject at the University of Poppleton[1]. Of course, this injustice is mitigated if the degree from Poppleton turns out to be less well regarded than the one from Liverpool, for then the expectation that this is the same qualification is at least partially removed. But we are not in that position – not exactly – and there are good reasons for resisting it anyway. Even where the universities in question are apparently of the same prestige, considerable problems concerning the establishment of common standards in a subject arise, as we have noted already, from differences in paradigm and tradition. This is to say neither that, therefore, there can be no standards nor that anything goes, because paradigms and traditions are constituted precisely by standards: a tradition depends on a community of scholars engaged in a common pursuit, and there can be no common pursuit without some criteria, explicit or non-explicit, for what counts as engagement in that pursuit. The idea of an academic pursuit is scarcely intelligible without there being some sense of what it is to engage in it well or badly. Standards are internal to the very notion of a discipline. What is needed to maintain standards then is above all the sustaining of such communities of scholars.

At the same time this is to present the picture too simply, as if such communities were more or less discrete and more or less stable. It is part of the practicalities of university life that staff do not operate in hermetic cells (however much the few may seek to isolate themselves in ever narrower specialisms): they are required to teach on a variety of courses and to collaborate with colleagues with different interests; they are called upon to contribute to research projects that may not be central to their concerns or their specialisms; their contacts go beyond the discipline they most identify with. It is part of the vitality of any tradition, moreover, that it should run up against disparate ways of doing and understanding things and that it should develop and change. Subject boundaries are breaking down, it is sometimes claimed, sometimes with a suggestion of epochal significance. Some see this as warranting a radical scepticism about the possibility of knowledge or the assertion of value, some as the legitimation of constructivism. In his inaugural lecture, *Realizing the University*, Ronald Barnett argues that the university must now dispense with key concepts that have variously organized it in the past. He groups these in the 'constellations' of knowledge and truth, production, democracy, emancipation, and the self. Each of these, Barnett argues, offers a grand narrative, and two problems arise from this. The first is that the narratives conflict, with no hope of resolution, the second that each relies on 'some sureness, some sense of stability, some sense of the enduring' when none is available in the modern world (Barnett, 1997a: 8). We have to accept that we are now in an era of change and uncertainty and the modern university is condemned to live with incoherence. In place of these Barnett invokes a 'constellation of fragility' encompassing uncertainty, unpredictability, challengeability, and contestability:

> While their emphases vary, these four ideas exhibit a number of features. First, they contain both cognitive *and* experiential aspects; second, they indicate the possibility of an undermining from the material world, from the world of human agency and from the world of ideas;

and third, they speak to an openness in our capacity to act in the world as well as to understand it. (Barnett, 1997a: 10)

In an age of supercomplexity the university must enable students to realize that the frameworks with which we might seek to understand the world are themselves challengeable: 'Creating uncertainty in the minds and beings of students and living effectively with this radical uncertainty: that is the double task of higher learning'. (Barnett, 1997a: 19).

But these are excessive reactions to a world that is changing faster than one had been inclined to accept, reactions of dismay at the loss of what was presumed to be certainty. What is crucial is not the issue of certainty but rather the value of the vocabularies and ways of understanding that academic subjects provide. These are characterized less by bodies of truths than by methods of enquiry and critique, with their own divisions and conflicts and with their own *avant-garde*.

Barnett is right to draw attention to the erosion of boundaries, both institutional and academic. If the boundaries between subjects are less clear than they were, this might instead lead us to a recognition of complexity and to ways in which subjects themselves can develop more fruitfully in interaction with what is other to them. It might provide a rationale for interdisciplinary approaches, which Dearing is concerned to support in some respects, but if our arguments about the role of academic communities are sound, the implication must be that such work arises against a background of initiation into disciplines. That there is some seepage between disciplines does not undermine the histories of their achievements nor render irrelevant the shared texts and interpretations that focus their debates; it does not invalidate the critical purchase that their distinctive vocabularies and perspectives provide.

We are arguing then that any coherent notion of academic standards must be grounded in those academic communities through which the disciplines have developed, that there is no firm ground outside these practices from which they might be judged. The ground that they provide is partially unstable and it shifts, but it offers nevertheless the continuities without which the enterprise of higher education would scarcely make sense.

It is clear, however, that the kind of common ground that is sought by Dearing is of a different order from that evident in the communities of scholars described above. The faint-heartedness concerning the possibility of identifying standards in the substance of courses, and perhaps a certain loss of faith in their intrinsic value, causes a turning of the attention to more general qualities and skills that relate to the procedural aspects of higher education. Dearing's endorsement of the idea of 'graduateness' promoted by the Higher Education Quality Council further reveals this. For this, it is held, 'could provide a common language and understanding about standards of awards at different levels' (10.92). This is sometimes given the distinctive imprimatur of the particular university but more central to the notion is the range of general abilities and transferable skills that the particular course is deemed to have provided. In the example of a 'completed programme specification template' provided in *Higher Quality* (QAA, 1998: 20–1) the main purposes of the course described – a multidisciplinary modular course in Sport, Coaching and Exercise Science – include the aim 'To develop critical and analytical problem solving skills and general/transferable skills to prepare students for more general graduate employment'. Of the four categories of learning outcome ('What a graduate should know and be able to do on completion of the programme'), two are almost entirely non-subject specific in their formulation. Thus under 'cognitive skills' the candidate is required to:

- Demonstrate the skills necessary to plan, conduct and report a programme of original research.
- Synthesize information/data from a variety of sources.
- Analyse, evaluate/interpret human performance.
- Apply biomechanical, physiological and psychological principles and methodologies to the solution of problems.
- Formulate and test concepts and hypotheses.

Under 'general/transferable skills (including key skills)' the candidate must demonstrate:

- Capacity to learn (in familiar/unfamiliar situations).
- Communicate effectively (written, verbal, graphical…).
- Numerical skills appropriate to the scientist.
- Competent use of Information Technology (eg WP, www, databases, spreadsheets, specialist packages).
- Able [sic] to work as part of a team.
- Able to work independently.

One thing to remark on about these lists is the proportion of the learning outcomes taken up by those that are classed as general and transferable.

The other is the vagueness of the aims. It is no exaggeration to say that the list is little different from those produced over a number of years now for low level further education courses run by City & Guilds. Compare the following from the Certificate in Pre-Vocational Education (CPVE, 1985):

12 CAREER PLAN
12.1 Can recognise the need for a personal career plan.
12.2 Can identify factors influencing local job opportunities.
12.3 Can make a realistic assessment of own career potential.
12.4 Can produce a personal career plan.

31 LISTENING
31.1 Can listen and respond to information presented in familiar situations.
31.2 Can listen and respond to information presented in a variety of situations.
31.3 Can select, interpret, and respond to information relevant to a particular purpose.

62 APPLICATION OF SCIENCE AND TECHNOLOGY TO PROBLEMS
62.1 Can identify problems capable of scientific or technical solution.
62.2 Can analyse problems capable of scientific or technical solution.
62.3 Can suggest appropriate solutions to technical or scientific problems.

Let us pass by the problems raised by the CPVE list, similar as they are to those in the QAA's.[2] What, in the latter, counts as the capacity to learn? And what constitutes an unfamiliar situation? What of the ability to communicate *effectively*? These specifications are little more than meaningless without reference to the substance of what is being learned. Even with the apparently more sophisticated cognitive skills above, or when one looks at the 'qualities, skills and capabilities profile' (critical reasoning, understanding/applying concepts, problem solving... independence/self-reliance, good learning skills, enterprise and resourcefulness) so much will depend on the particular level at which the tasks are set and the student is operating (QAA, 1998: 20). Without this the specifications are tantamount to useless.

In fact, they are worse than useless because they have the superficial appearance of rigour and objectivity – they seem just what we need in order to restore standards. It is typical of the way that universities are currently being encouraged to emulate practices that have put down their roots in further education, and that have already constricted its flourishing. There are some things that universities can learn from further education colleges, but the scientistic language of curriculum intention demonstrated here is not one of them. The reverse of the safeguarding of standards, this is the universities' dumbing down.

Against the crass vacuousness of some of the abilities listed above, the aim that students gain competence with information technology seems relatively uncontentious, and we do not suggest that this is not good sense. Again there are problems with the lack of specification of the levels demanded. But we raise a different point here. This is that the kinds of ability needed would not be very sophisticated and would be fairly easily acquired. Probably many students in schools and colleges will have gained abilities at these levels before embarking on the course. Hence there is a danger that excessive credit is attached to what are not necessarily high level abilities in the overall profile of the degree. Insofar as this element were to take the place of credit given for knowledge and understanding in the subject, this would again constitute a reduction in standards, however marketable this might be with employers and however attractive to students.

The final point we make about these specifications of skills, one which relates to the notion of graduateness more generally, has to do with how far these profiles exert a normalizing effect on learners. Would it be desirable, for example, if all students demonstrated enterprise and resourcefulness, teamwork, 'client focus'? Do all students, for that matter, need to be active learners in the sense that they speak up in seminars and take the initiative? If so there is a restriction on the ways that people can approach a subject that may in the end be inhibiting for that subject. The student who sits in silence may be more strenuously challenged and more thoughtful in her response than the person who joins in with the discussion 'actively'. More generally, and more insidiously, a certain norm of human behaviour, one devised partly with an eye on employment, comes to be imposed on those who enter universities. Customer satisfaction starts to look more like a matter of the artificial creation of desire: the student sees herself as someone who selects modules, learns actively, and acquires competencies – this after all is what education is.

What the QAA is doing with documents such as *Higher Quality* appears to be in line with the recommendations of the CVCP. It argues that priorities for the QAA should include assisting the sector to agree benchmarks and a qualifications framework, and the piloting of systems for reporting on achievement of threshold standards across the sector

(CVCP, 1998: para. 22). We see some sense in this but at the same time are suspicious of the faith that may be placed in it. When we examine students, we do this on the strength of familiarity with students' work, built up over time. If we are new to the game, we draw on the experience of others. The good examiner draws on that experience and not on a checklist. Checklists are sufficient for some types of performance but this is not generally true of the kinds of study that rightfully go on in universities. Thus this accumulated shared experience, central to the teaching of a subject, is a rich resource even if it is one that by its very nature cannot easily be spelt out or made transparent. Where checklists such as grade descriptors are drawn up, they draw from this well of experience of judgement in practice, and in their application they rely on an appropriateness of interpretation that that experience makes possible. Explicit formulation, however, can mislead us into thinking that they themselves are the authoritative source and final safeguard of standards. We contend, furthermore, that where there is an attempt to specify threshold standards and benchmarks rigorously this may well lead to a lowering of standards. The reasons for this are twofold: first, anxieties about rigour are likely to cause such standards to be expressed in unduly behavioural terms; and second, they are likely to give the impression that this is all a student needs to do, and so to reduce the inclination to acknowledge and reward what has not been anticipated.

In the quest for common standards or for general qualities of graduateness, the variety of human learning and experience is in danger of neglect, so too in teaching and examining the central importance of practical experience can be undervalued. This was already evident in the MacFarlane Report (CSUP, 1992) into higher education in Scotland which seems in miniature to have sketched the kind of picture that Dearing has worked to. MacFarlane's faith was placed in a combination of new technology in hand with a particular psychology of learning. Differences in subjects or in people paled in the face of the streamlined system that was envisaged. It is important that the new Institute for Learning and Teaching in Higher Education does not make similar mistakes. The prevailing vision is one of the tidy specification of courses, clearly defined outcomes, and mission statements in aid of transparency and presentation – streamlined process (running like a well-oiled machine) to the neglect of (the difficulties of) content. Seeing things in terms of process in the ways we have detailed in this chapter generates the idea that for every activity there is a correct procedure or technique. Thus more and more of our lives is invaded by this normalizing process. It is not that other behaviour is outlawed; rather there is a presumption of correct method that guides us and channels us from the start. In part this is an expansion of a certain manifestation of rationality. It exerts on us a requirement of totalizing our conception of ourselves, though this may be brought under the more attractive rubrics of, say, autonomy or independence or teamwork.

It is a conception of rationality, moreover that assumes that we must have an explicit idea of what we are doing. In 1950 Michael Oakeshott showed remarkable prescience when he spoke with concern of the way talk of the mission of the university was spreading (Fuller, 1989: 96). It is a mistake, Oakeshott argued, to suppose that having a mission in life involves determining a goal and then calculating how to act to realize that goal. Rather it is the other way about: it involves knowing how to behave in a certain way and in trying to behave in that way. 'Mission' will then be a kind of shorthand expression of this knowledge and behaviour; it will not be a programme – or the basis of a programme – of action. The point is underscored by the famous analogy between educational practice and a kind of conversation. The good conversation is not praised for its end result so much as for its intrinsic quality. A university is not a contrivance of some sort with a particular function, appropriately stipulated by a statement of intent. To see it in such terms is already to have thrown something valuable away.

Oakeshott's words may cause us to reflect on the possibility that the historic achievement of our higher education was put together not by managers with business plans and mission statements but by men 'who dimly knew what they did', beckoned on by aims higher than they could easily imagine, seeking a perfection of human nature by adding to it what is more than nature, and directing it towards aims higher than its own (Fuller, 1989: 48–9). These are uncomfortable and untimely thoughts perhaps. The humility here, more pervasively appropriate in higher education than these remarks can suggest, is rarely in evidence in the policy documents of today.

'PROGRESSIVE' MANAGERIALISM

It is, of course, quite unsurprising, if not perfectly natural, that the development of a mass higher education system should arouse expectations that the system should be managed, and the proliferation of courses reinforces this impression. Of course, management itself is a matter of procedure. The growing awareness of the dangers of the rationalization of society that exists in post-industrial societies sits incongruously with managerialism of the sort that Dearing promotes. But a similar element of contradiction is evident in the way that the development of information technologies has led to both increasing possibilities of central control and opportunities for enhancing local democratic initiatives. With both new technology and the instrumentalism of managerialism, however, the imprint of technology on human experience is increasingly felt. In the twentieth century the sustaining narratives and moral certainties of former ages were replaced by scientific certainties but these also reached towards a metadiscourse from which judgements could be substantiated. It may be that social change has helped to undermine a misplaced confidence in this metadiscourse but it is not itself a matter of social change: the issue is deeper.

It is the reaction to the absence of this kind of metadiscourse or to the ultimate certainties needed, so it is supposed, to securely ground our knowledge that leads to the scepticism and relativism that we have cited. Alternatively, and as with Dearing, the reaction so characteristic of modern managerialism is the retreat towards the procedural, and this leaves the suspicion of an evasion, if not a fundamental lack of confidence in the credibility, of commitments to any values (other than those of the very instrumentalism that perpetuates the problem).

The emphasis on procedural values compensates for the loss of (the centrality of) substance by imagining us as disengaged agents who *operate* on the world (which is independent of our ways of thinking about it). It takes our developing knowledge to be a technology (and in passing fails to grasp well the nature of technology), an operation by a subject on the objects of the world. There are surreptitious effects to this hegemony of technology, revealed, for example, in the difficulty people have in thinking in anything other than instrumental terms – in terms of the mantra of resources, efficiency and effectiveness, usefulness, cost-benefit analysis.

It is a curious consequence of the focus on the procedural that the kind of higher education that is being promoted is ironically reminiscent of the progressivism of primary education in the late 1960s and 1970s. Curious because the received wisdom in education regarding progressivism is captured by John Major's adage that the progressives have had their say and they have had their day. Yet here in the jargon of lifelong learning the focus of the new higher education must be on the learners themselves. In the 1960s R S Peters criticized child-centred education for its excessive concern with the manner rather than the matter of education. The new 'progressivism' in higher education has only a veneer of the concern with personal growth and creativity that characterized the primary education of the *Plowden Report* or the *Primary Memorandum*. Underneath this can easily be seen the drive to prepare people 'effectively' for work. The language of learner-centredness has readily been harnessed to a consumerist conception of empowerment, where the positioning of learners as isolated choosers renders more achievable the streamlined flexible systems upon which managerialism thrives, and the surreptitious creation of desire. It can be seen, nevertheless, that our charge is similar to Peters's: that it is the neglect of the substance of higher education that leads to the most significant distortions that current policy is effecting. Neglect of the matter of higher education is a blindness to what a university education must surely be about.

CONCLUSION

We said earlier in the chapter that we would return to the question of whether anything can be established concerning general criteria for a course's appropriateness at university level. Diversification has undermined the criteria that were in the past tacitly assumed. We have little sympathy for the assumption that this tacit understanding should simply be replaced by a precise code or specification because we take the view that the development of such understanding is the result of accumulated shared experience, shared precisely through those academic communities and networks of external examiners of which we have made much in this chapter. On the other hand, we do not think that nothing can be said, and we suggest the following. A subject fit for study at degree level then should have these characteristics:

1. It must embody a tradition of enquiry in which there are continuities in the sets of problems and in the methods of research, although there will be disagreement about these. Hence it is essentially public in character.
2. It must involve the study of sets of texts that are shared by practitioners of the subject as common reference points, although there will be disagreement about these texts and there need be no canonical list.
3. Crucially it will involve the exercise of critical judgement in relation to the objects of enquiry, but this will be evident also in a recurrent introspection about the nature of the subject in question. Thus the tradition will incorporate dissent not only over methods of procedure but over the nature and purpose of the enquiry itself.

4. Such criticism and dissent will make sense in the light of those continuities, and it will be possible in virtue of the critical vocabularies that the discipline provides. Studying the subject involves an initiation into those critical vocabularies.

5. Whether vocational or 'purely academic', a subject must be of intrinsic interest and always worthy of further pursuit. This is not, of course, to say that it will necessarily or always be pursued in that way but it must incorporate subject matter that is potentially fascinating, whether or not it has a pay-off in terms of its ultimate usefulness.

6. However specialized, a subject must have a bearing on life as a whole. It cannot like a game have no significance beyond the pursuit in question.

7. It must have an unlimited capacity to develop.

This is not, it need hardly be said, a tidy checklist. Above all it requires interpretation. We believe, however, not only that the list offers an appropriate guide to the qualities a subject requires to be worthy of inclusion in the university curriculum but that it highlights qualities that should be promoted. Some of these, we suggest, will not be promoted where the emphasis is on the apparently more rigorous attempts at specification that are currently advocated.

At the beginning of this chapter we suggested that two principles underpin the drive for wider participation in higher education: the need for largely economic reasons for a more highly educated population and the extension of opportunity in such a way as to empower individuals. We take both these principles to be appropriate to higher education and indeed laudable, but both need to be understood in terms rather different from those that prevail in Dearing and more generally in the contemporary debate.

There is currently an excessive emphasis on the need for a more highly educated population, exacerbated no doubt by the crisis in funding that has inevitably arisen as participation has widened. But more generally this is driven by the climate of instrumentalism, where quality assurance is closely related to the idea of a return on investment, which has been illustrated in the various chapters of this book. Quality assurance, as by now must be clear, judges things in terms of an interchangeability that is ultimately reductive of the distinctive features, the peculiar goods, of different things. It submits things to a common standard (How reassuring the phrase is!) and to a measurement of performance (Objectivity at last!). When the notion of quality is examined more closely, however, it seems that it involves understanding whatever is to count as of value in terms of what will survive in the market place. Thus, in the work of Roger Ellis it seems that in public services such as health and education it is the consumer who has the final say and that services are thereby subjected to a kind of survival of the fittest. Bill Hart's response is refreshing:

> 'Quality', according to Ellis, 'Is that which gives complete customer satisfaction' (Ellis, 1988, p 7). Well there's a thought to ponder. *Quality is that which gives complete customer satisfaction.* A top quality dishwasher is one that satisfies the customer. Completely. A middling dishwasher is one that satisfies the customer in some ways but not in others. A poor dishwasher is … (you get the picture). Ditto for service in a restaurant. The more satisfied the customer is the better the service: the less satisfied the customer the worse the service. Man – *qua* customer – is the measure of all things. 'The definition holds for every customer, housewife, industrial buyer or hospital patient' (Ellis, *ibid*.). But really Ellis is here understating his case. For if what he is offering is truly a *definition* of 'quality' then it must apply across the board. It can't just be 'quality products' and 'quality services' which give complete customer satisfaction, but quality and goodness in all its forms. A good book will be one people in general won't regret buying, a good concert one which will give them *their money's worth*. A good sunset (I suppose) is one which is well worth paying to see. And a good neighbour or friend…? Truth to tell, I don't know *what* Professor Ellis wants me to say here.
>
> The Professor's reduction of our judgements of value to a kind of *Which* Report with an emphasis on the Best Buy is, I would like to think, cheerfully crass. A joke which anyone could see the funny side of. If someone emerged from a performance of *King Lear* and declared he had got his money's worth – declared himself, that's to say, a fully satisfied customer – what would we conclude but that he hadn't really *seen* the play; that it was *wasted* on him? What would we make of a mother who – wishing to praise hospital staff who had done their best, unsuccessfully, to save the life of her child – said that they had given value for money? What would we think of doctors for whom *that* was the ultimate accolade? The minute we begin to take Ellis's proposed definition of quality seriously we enter into complicity with ways of speaking which, at the first breath of contact with life, we immediately feel to be incongruous or comic. (Hart, 1997: 297–8)

This means that the sense that can be given to such notions as the public good is skewed from the start. The good is understood primarily in terms of economic prosperity, with its measurable financial indicators, and more or less uncritically. Of course, there will remain debates over the just distribution of wealth (and the very real questions of injustice that these raise can themselves sometimes hide from us our evasion of questions of value). But wealth itself is conceived in abstract monetary terms. Once again any consideration of the substantive goods that might arise from this wealth, that might be its point, is elided in favour of the preoccupation with money – the means, indeed the procedure, of its exchange. In a similar way the idea of the public is understood in terms of the aggregate of individuals who make up society (if such, in these impoverished terms, can still be presumed to exist). It is a short step then to the idea that democratic participation consists primarily in voting, in political elections, of course, but also in those other opportunities for choice that the technology of our time increasingly makes possible, and the extension of which inevitably reinforces the very conception of democracy that is at issue. The provision of structures that offer students more opportunities for choice in higher education is not unrelated to this. If at the political level this involves an erosion of the public sphere, so also in education what is learnt becomes partially severed from the public realm in which it has its real life. For, as we have demonstrated, educational goods are essentially the products of shared traditions of thought and enquiry, and induction into them is an initiation into these public modes of thought and enquiry. To pursue a subject is at some level to engage in a conversation, and this presupposes that somewhere there is a community that sustains this. This renders all the more odd – even incoherent – the prevailing picture of isolated learners that we criticize in Chapter 5. To put the emphasis on the accessing and manipulation of data runs the risk of consigning the flickering perception of this community to the periphery of the learner's vision, even as it needs to be focused and made more vivid. In the process it obscures the sense of what the public realm might be.

It follows from this that whatever wealth accrues to the learner as a result of her efforts she will be empowered only in a limited sense. She will be a free agent able to exercise her autonomous choice in the market place perhaps but she will have no grasp of that public world that the agora might otherwise enshrine. Her mind will have been informed by the skills and competencies, by the proficiency with information technology, that shape and equip her for the instrumental world she is likely to confront. She will come to think of what it is to be educated as itself a matter of accumulated course units and profiles of skills. Rather than being empowered she will be consigned to these limitations for the very skills she acquires, and their tidy fit with the curriculum outcomes her

courses aim at, occlude the public realm that the academic subject ultimately must rely on. The point is not just that her initiation into and participation in the subject will be restricted but that through this her
conception of and participation in the public world will be curtailed; and
as a result of this she will contribute less to that public world, because
participation will depend on a vivid sense of the nature and the point of
that shared activity, and this she will not have. It will depend precisely
on not seeing the public as the aggregate of individuals but rather as the
vital source for any properly human existence. It is an impoverished
idea of service to society that does not take this into account. Engagement with the substance of academic subjects is a public good.

We said at the start of this chapter that empowerment may be understood to incorporate a robust conception of citizenship where students
take on the role of contributing to the development and shaping of their
society in ways that are in part expressive of themselves but through
which they in some sense find themselves. We have now tried to show
how the kind of empowerment, the private benefit, that the individual
might gain from higher education is not separable from the public good.
There is a reciprocal connection here but one that is distorted by the contractual terms that now tend to be adopted. The point is not that individuals engage in a collaborative exercise where each is contracted for a
particular role; the point is rather that my prosperity partially consists in
yours. I am already out there in the public space with you, and higher
education provides a means, perhaps the best means, for our mutual
flourishing. It is from the communal goods of academic subjects that the
private goods and public benefits of higher education derive.

Notes

1. The fictional and somewhat less than prestigious University of
   Poppleton figures regularly in Laurie Taylor's weekly column in the
   Times Higher Educational Supplement.
2. For a fuller discussion of the language of curriculum objectives, see
   Standish (1991).

3

Aims, Purposes and Principles

What does Dearing think higher education is *for*? In this chapter we ask this very basic question, and evaluate the answer, or rather answers, that Dearing gives. We also go a little further, asking what kind of a question Dearing thinks this is, and how Dearing thinks we should go about answering it. We speculate on whether the graduates of a post-Dearing university would be better or worse able to consider such a question than previous generations. This is not because we think that the purpose of universities is to enable consideration of what universities are for. Such self-reference and circularity is rightly found in certain kinds of novel-writing, not in the real world. Yet imagine that the question was asked in such a way, or that the terms in which answers were framed were set in such a way, that eventually only certain kinds of answer could be given. Imagine for example a report on higher education which reduced all the rich and diverse kinds of knowing and understanding to the 'information' that can be stored in and transmitted via electronic technology (of course Dearing does not do this: such a reduction awaits a future report). This would be a reason for concern. Our resources for thinking about higher education would have been narrowed down just as surely, and perhaps just as disastrously, as our biological resources are diminished when swathes of rain-forest are destroyed. We do not think things have got to this point in Dearing, but we do indicate what we think are some worrying developments.

AIMS

We start elsewhere, away from what may appear the Anglo-Saxon common sense of Dearing (the man, as distinct from his Report, has after all acquired the reputation of the arch-fixer, the pragmatist). Developments in higher education in Europe cast an interesting light on what is happening in the UK. In the pages of the 1995 European White Paper, 'Teaching and Learning: Towards the Learning Society', there can be found a confident and remarkable declaration on the question of what education is for:

> Everyone is convinced of the need for change, the proof being the demise of the major ideological disputes on the objectives of education.

Elsewhere (p 24) a section is entitled 'The end of debate on educational principles'. Here, then, the question of what higher education is for has been abolished, as it were, by bureaucratic decree. This is serious news for anyone who likes to think that the fundamental questions, about education as well as about anything else in life, repay constant revisiting and reassessing. How did its authors reach this conclusion?

This White Paper explicitly develops and takes forward another, 'Growth, Competitiveness, Employment', which stressed the importance for Europe of 'intangible investment, particularly in education and training' (European Commission, 1995: 1). In its conclusion, 'Teaching and Learning' compares the challenges facing Europe today with those of the Middle Ages and the post-medieval period when there was competition with the Byzantine, Arab and Ottoman spheres of influence: now, 'Teaching and Learning' says, our competitors, with whom we are engaged in 'struggle', are 'America, Japan and soon China' (European Commission, 1995: 53). The language of economic competition becomes that of almost militaristic threat. Yet this began with talk of a learning society: a vision, one might think, of people coming together for edification in communal endeavour. Discussion of what education is for, then – of its aims, ends or purposes – has been dissolved in a general assumption that education exists to serve the economy, of the nation or community of nations, presumably, as political circumstances change.

Now what of Dearing? Chapter 5 is subtitled 'Aims and purposes'. Three paragraphs set out a brief history of the issue, and remind us of the four aims and objectives of the Robbins Report of 1963. Then, under the heading 'Our views', Dearing sets out (5.11) what it sees as the four main purposes of higher education:

■ to inspire and enable individuals to develop their capabilities to the highest potential levels throughout life, so that they grow intellectually, are well-equipped for work, can contribute effectively to society and achieve personal fulfilment;

- to increase knowledge and understanding for their own sake and to foster their application to the benefit of the economy and society;
- to serve the needs of an adaptable, sustainable, knowledge-based economy at local, regional and national levels;
- to play a major role in shaping a democratic, civilised, inclusive society.

Now this is admirably straightforward, it may appear. The first two points balance the intrinsic merits of personal development and the growth of knowledge and understanding with their extrinsic benefits for the labour market and society more widely. The third point unambiguously states that one of the functions of higher education is to meet the needs of the economy (a point, we should say here and now, that we do not dissent from) and the last point reshapes Robbins's fourth objective, 'the transmission of a common culture and common standards of citizenship', into an expression of purpose which is arguably better suited to a society grown even more pluralistic and diverse, more fissiparous, than it was in 1963.

Yet it is important to notice that these 'purposes' are subsumed under an overarching 'aim'. (Robbins talked of the 'aims' of higher education, but only prefaced discussion of its 'objectives' by saying how complex they were and how difficult to balance.) Dearing's overarching aim of higher education is 'to enable society to make progress through an understanding of itself and its world' (Dearing: 5.10). Better and better, one might think, especially in view of what we write in our opening paragraph above. What could be more noble than that higher education should help to create a society so reflective and self-critical that even higher education's role in it should always be open to scrutiny? However, there is a crucial gloss. The words just quoted from para. 5.10 are followed by: 'in short, to sustain a learning society'. So is this what a learning society is: one that makes 'progress through an understanding of itself and its world'? Is it also, or is it rather, something else?

Here it is important to refer to the opening words of Dearing's Chapter 1, which is entitled 'A vision for 20 years: the learning society':

> 1.1 The purpose of education is life-enhancing: it contributes to the whole quality of life. This recognition of the purpose of higher education in the development of our people, our society, and our economy is central to our vision. In the next century, the economically successful nations will be those which become learning societies: where all are committed, through effective education and training, to lifelong learning.

1.2 So, to be a successful nation in a competitive world, and to maintain a cohesive society and a rich culture, we must invest in education to develop our greatest resource, our people. The challenge to achieve this through the excellence and effectiveness of education is great...

There is a danger here of overstating our case and, some will perhaps object, of reading too much in here. But the words say what they say. A balanced set of 'purposes', broadly reminiscent of Robbins's 'objectives', and perhaps destined to be what is remembered of Dearing in the same way as Robbins's objectives are the most widely-quoted part of his report, are held to constitute a 'learning society'. But the opening paragraphs of the substance of the Report, the first elements of the 20-year vision, make it clear that, in some unspecified way, 'life-enhancing' and 'quality of life' translate above all into economic success, competitiveness and 'effectiveness'. Compare para. 1.10:

1.10 The expansion of higher education in the last ten years has contributed greatly to the creation of a learning society, that is, a society in which people in all walks of life recognise the need to continue in education and training throughout their working lives and who see learning as enhancing the quality of life throughout all its stages. But, looking twenty years ahead, the UK must progress further and faster in the creation of such a society to sustain a competitive economy.

What in the recent past has been seen as enhanced quality of life will in the future become a matter of economic competitiveness. Para. 1.11 expands on this with familiar talk of the global economy, the pace of innovation and people as the best resources for securing competitive advantage. There is more than a suggestion here that if you don't accept Dearing's analysis you'll find that the company you work for has transferred its operations to the Philippines.

It is impossible to write these criticisms, muted and oblique as they are, without seeming to hear the kind of response that has become almost automatic. 'This is the real world – and a new and rapidly changing world. Unless higher education accepts its responsibility to prepare students to meet the new challenges and opportunities, equipping them with the skills and knowledge that are needed, there will not be the degree of national prosperity to sustain anyone in the enhanced quality of life, non-materialistic or materialistic, that we all value'. So it is worth repeating that we have no problem with the idea that one purpose – even a major purpose – of higher education is to sustain and improve the nation's standard of living.

We are not simply making the point that Dearing has overemphasized the extrinsic, economic pay-off of higher education, or that the report has insinuated repeated reference to such benefits under cover of the broader and more liberal-sounding ideal of a 'learning society'. Our criticism is more complex. It seems to us that a number of factors, each on its own relatively harmless, have combined in Dearing to guarantee the final triumph of instrumental thinking, whose most familiar modern form is the valuing of economic success. These factors, which are interconnected and difficult to separate from each other, are the language of instrumental reason, the assumption of individualism and the thinning of our conception of a person, and the failure to devote proper thought to questions of ends (questions of aims and purposes), including the ends of higher education.

INSTRUMENTAL REASON

Instrumental reason (see also Chapter 5) is sometimes called technical or scientific reason or rationality. Its realm is the discovery of the best means to ends which are known and specified in advance: finding what blend of foodstuff will maximize pork production, or what is the best temperature for a piece of machinery to run at if it is not to break down. In education technical reason is employed to try to establish appropriate pay levels for teachers and lecturers (no point in raising pay unless you are short of qualified personnel), or to work out the least time-consuming way of communicating messages to a large group of students. As Martha Nussbaum puts it, it is concerned with 'the management of need and with prediction and control concerning future contingencies' (Nussbaum, 1986: 95). Technical reason produces rules and procedures; it increases our power to make universal rather than particular statements, for example about the best way of communicating with all relevantly similar large groups of students. It helps us to achieve a high degree of precision and to construct explanations that help us to refine our rules and procedures still further (cp Nussbaum, 1986: 95-6).

Technical reason has done a great deal to make our lives longer and more comfortable. For instance, it is technical reason that a researcher uses when she works out which drugs, and in what amounts, quickly and safely reduce inflammation or kill pain. As this example shows, however, even in the areas of its most spectacular successes technical reason on its own is not enough. Medical experiments on the mentally handicapped are not an acceptable way of trialling new drugs, and it is not technical thinking that tells us this but thinking of the ethical kind. The trouble is that the achievements of technical reason in the areas to which it is appropriate – the development of technology, for example, particularly information technology – have been so remarkable that there is the constant risk of its power and its methods spreading into areas where its use is inappropriate or needs to be tempered with other forms of thinking. As Martha Nussbaum (1990: 55) writes, 'the power of "scientific" pictures of practical rationality affects almost every area of human social life, through the influence of the social sciences and the more science-based parts of ethical theory on the formation of public policy'.

It was during the Enlightenment and the scientific revolutions of the seventeenth and eighteenth centuries that technical and instrumental rationality began to achieve the dominance that we now tend to take for granted. Its critics however (such as Horkheimer and Adorno and, more recently, Jurgen Habermas) have long argued that the power of technical reason to predict and control has, for all its benefits, brought in its train sophisticated forms of manipulation and enslavement. For an obvious example, consider how new computer technology enables us to store and retrieve enormous amounts of information. This creates a demand for the supply of such information that in itself places demands (on academics, in the context of higher education). In turn the information makes possible, and thus somehow inevitable, the league-tables and performance indicators which create extra stress for those who find themselves and their organizations (universities and university departments) ranked and graded. In this way technical reason both liberates and oppresses. Our fundamental human need to understand and communicate with each other, and our interest in setting ourselves free from our dependence on the world around us (Habermas, 1978), are things which technical reason cannot meet.

Currently education is heavily dominated by the technicist model of rationality. It can be seen in the insistence that quality in schooling can be measured, benchmarked and raised ('levered up', in a revealing phrased favoured by Kenneth Baker when he was Education Minister) by the setting of targets. The school curriculum has for some while now been seen as something that can be 'delivered', with the corollary assumption that once content is specified purely instrumental questions can be asked about the best method of delivery. Both in schooling and in higher education one of the surest symptoms of 'technical reason syndrome' is the way that talk of effectiveness is everywhere. We give some examples of this in Chapter 5. Talk of effectiveness is a clear sign that technical reason is asserting its grip. To be effective is all about means, about getting to a goal as cheaply, certainly or reliably as possible. It says nothing about whether that goal is worth getting to; often the refrain of 'effectiveness' and 'efficiency' operates as a good way of concealing that no real thought has been given to questions of ends, or that, as in the example from the European White Paper cited above, questions of ends are taken to be solved, misconceived or redundant.

Notice the way Dearing deploys 'effectiveness'. The word occurs twice in the opening two paragraphs quoted above, reinforcing the sense that of all the aims of education it is the economic one that really matters: '… the economically successful nations will be those… where all are committed, through *effective* education and training, to lifelong learning' (1.1, our emphasis). Economic success will require education geared to just that: the disguised tautology prevents us asking the questions that we might want to ask if we were told that the nation's future requires that education take economic success as its principal goal. (Isn't the future importantly about other values too, many of which cannot be measured in economic terms? Anyway, is it even obvious what kind of education the drive for economic success would require?)

It is often worth asking what talk of effectiveness *adds*. Look again at the first of Dearing's 'four main purposes of higher education'. Individuals are to be inspired and enabled so that they can 'contribute effectively to society'. As soon as we press the word we see that either it is meaningless, adding nothing, or it carries firm-jawed, steely-eyed associations of making a difference, getting things done. At which point of course we want to observe that not all differences are worth making (Hitler was a highly effective leader, and made a great difference to Europe), not all things are to be got done. Effectiveness is the language of action regardless of value. Mrs Thatcher, famously, praised David (later Lord) Young on the grounds that where other people brought her problems he came to her with solutions. Along somewhat similar lines a professor of education recently complained (*Times Higher Education Supplement*, 22 May 1998, p 2: 'Research hurts teaching') that 'British educational research is often "highly damaging" to teacher effectiveness'. He blames higher education for failing to view teaching as an 'applied science', and attributes the stubborn refusal of schooling standards to rise to 'the research establishment's "virtual total ignorance" of teacher effectiveness'. The link between technical reason, here present in the hankering for the authority and prestige of the status of 'applied science', and the slogan of 'effectiveness' could hardly be more clear.

There is nothing particularly new in the claim that technical or instrumental reason has come to dominate talk about higher education, as many other parts of our world. Ronald Barnett, for instance, has made this a theme of many of his analyses of higher education. In *The Limits of Competence* (1994), for example, he writes:

> higher education is being locked into a Weberian iron cage of prescriptive rationality, of given ends and of operationalism... in its various forms – bureaucratic, purposive, strategic and technocratic – instrumental reason so seeps into social institutions and human affairs generally that it becomes the dominant mode of reason. In the terminology of Jürgen Habermas, instrumental reason colonises the life-world, which would otherwise be the domain of open, interpersonal reason. Instead of engaging with each other and with the world in mutual interaction, we end up by always having an eye to the main chance and by getting out of our transactions with each other and with the world what we can get away with. (Barnett, 1994: 5, 78)

Yet, as this chapter has sought to illustrate, those who form policy in higher education show no signs of heeding the analysis. Worse than that, the grip of the 'iron cage' becomes more relentless with every report and official publication. (It is worth noting that Barnett, probably the best-known philosopher of higher education in the English-speaking world, was not included on the Dearing Committee.)

SKILLS

Another aspect of instrumental reason, and again one which Barnett himself draws attention to, is the prevalence of the language of 'skills'. 'Skills-talk', the tendency to call all manner of human knacks, abilities, competencies, capacities, qualities and virtues alike 'skills', is everywhere in current educational writing. There are, it is alleged, skills of everything under the sun, from greeting shop customers and stacking shelves to reading. There are parenting skills, lovemaking skills, even (a real example, from an examiner's report which unfortunately cannot be cited) the skills of self-knowledge. To see what is odd about all this talk of skills, we might look first at an example from another area of education. Writing of Personal and Social Education (PSE), the authors of *Education for Adult Life: the Spiritual and Moral Development of Young People* (SCAA, 1996: 15) declare:

> The value of PSE was seen by some in developing interpersonal skills, including managing feelings, understanding others and learning to take responsibility for one's actions.

This kind of vapid statement is now so common in writing about education that it is easy not to notice how odd it is.[1] What are 'interpersonal skills'? Aren't interpersonal relationships more a matter of what kind of *person* you are rather than what skills you deploy? If we are in trouble or distress, for instance, do we not value a friend who is a good listener – they *want* to give us their time and attention, it is not a matter of a technique which they can turn on at will – rather than someone with listening *skills*? As for 'managing feelings', there is something worrying about a person of whom you could say that he was skilled at managing his feelings. This sounds closer to dissembling, to maintaining a façade behind which one's real feelings cannot be seen, than to the kind of self-control and self-knowledge which the authors presumably have in mind. And what about 'learning to take responsibility for one's actions'? How could this be a skill which you exercise (with the implication that you could choose on occasion not to), rather than a matter of growing into a more mature kind of person?

Dearing contains some striking examples of skills-talk. Recommendation 21, for example, requires institutions of higher education to specify the intended outcomes of their programmes in terms of various skills, including the 'key skills' of communication and learning how to learn, and cognitive skills, 'such as an understanding of methodologies'. To take just the first of these: if my students have been learning to listen to each other in our seminars, to give each other space and neither to dominate discussion nor to interrupt each other, to exercise some tact and discretion in advancing their arguments, is this truly a matter of acquiring *skills*, or of developing moral qualities or even virtues? Or something more like, in Michael Oakeshott's famous phrase, learning to take part in a kind of conversation? Whether or not we think in terms of 'skills' here is far from being a merely verbal matter or a quibble. Learning to communicate is something to which we bring the whole of ourselves: our sincerity, commitment, personal values and other qualities (even *virtues*) are all at stake. To learn to communicate as a matter of practising skills or techniques, by contrast, is to learn to play on people's susceptibilities, to manipulate them and achieve certain *effects* (in this sense the skilled communicator is indeed effective). But presumably Dearing does not want us to teach our students to be sophists or rhetoricians.

The way that such 'skills-talk' actually unhinges the idea of education it is called upon to operationalize can be seen in a further passage from *Education for Adult Life* (p 11). Here there is talk of the need for schools to develop

> the skills that enable young people to make wise decisions and develop acceptable values, attitudes and behaviour ... we place too much emphasis on preparation for work and not enough on preparation for life, particularly self-development in terms of spiritual, physical, sexual, social, vocational and moral attributes and qualities. A practical recommendation was that any list of 'key skills' should include 'skills for life'. (SCAA, 1996: 11)

Here the moral life – self-development in terms of moral qualities, as the authors rather oddly put it – is itself seen as a matter of having the relevant skills. But how could morality be reduced to skills? The objections to this are amongst the most elementary moves in moral philosophy. First, a just or honest person is one who *wants* to be just and honest, who is disposed to be so: to have a skill, on the other hand, is to have something you can choose to exercise or not, or something which you can choose to exercise for bad rather than for good. The skilled doctor, as Plato observed, makes a good poisoner. Secondly, moral questions are about ends rather than about means. If you refrain from stealing as a means to not being imprisoned then this is clearly not a moral principle but a prudential one. Skills on the other hand pertain to means. That is just what a skill is, or was before recent confusion. The skilled technician sets up your new computer: he does not involve himself in your ends and question whether you would in fact be better off, live a richer and fuller life, without the new technology. Thirdly, the moral life entails commitment. Your qualities and virtues, or lack of them, tell people something about the sort of person you are. They go to make up your identity. Others do not know anything fundamental about you, however, when they know that you do or do not have the skill of using a word processor, of tuning your car engine or of raising geraniums from seed.

INDIVIDUALISM

The tendency to elevate skills and competencies to pride of place is one of the most individualizing factors at work in current thinking about education. For to cast qualities and abilities as skills is precisely to decontextualize them. If semi-literacy, for example, is a matter of having poor reading skills then responsibility is thereby removed from the family which treats books with hostility if not suspicion, and from a society which increasingly seems to regard them as either a hurdle on the road to qualifications or a means of escapism, not qualitatively different from a computer game, and attributed to the individual who has failed to acquire the relevant skills. If being a half-reasonable mother is a question of 'parenting skills' and not a function of the complex interrelationships between a woman, her children and the world they live in, then she ought to solve the problem by going off to acquire the skills she personally lacks, irrespective of the conditions under which she lives that might be connected with her lack of patience or the politicians who add guilt and anxiety to the demands of being a single mother. If lecturers and students ought to pay more attention to communication skills then there are some reassuringly self-contained moves to be made in order to acquire the appropriate techniques. The lecturer's stress (perhaps she has no stress management skills, and should go on a short course), occasioned by trying to meet publishers' deadlines while hunting for missing coursework and chasing research grants, the students' difficulty in maintaining full attention (most of them have worrying debts and part-time evening jobs not conducive to alertness at nine o'clock in the morning), the fact that the seminar room has desks bolted to the floor, in rows facing the front – all these contextual factors are to be ignored if what is at issue in learning to communicate is a matter of *skills*. And that we know these factors cannot be ignored, that they are somewhere near the heart of what is involved when we try to talk with each other openly and sensitively, is what makes it clear that we are not talking about true skills here at all.

Skills and competencies, then, seem to be something we attribute to the individual, ignoring (and perhaps in order to ignore, for political, practical or psychological reasons) the surrounding reasons why people can or cannot do this or that. Through this process of 'individualizing' our conception of individuals themselves is becoming ever thinner. This is what happens when we see learning essentially in terms of skills, for to insist on seeing the great range of human qualities and capacities as *skills* is to see them as connected only accidentally with those who possess them. A skill is something you can lack, or have, without it saying anything significant about *you*. If you couldn't do something it is just because you didn't have the skills. Lasch (1984) suggests that our love of 'skills-talk' is a way of protecting our fragile and threatened selves when times are difficult: we hold our skills, so to speak, at arm's length. Anything that reflects badly on them does not then have to reflect badly on our 'essential selves'. But this means, conversely, that skills understood in this way cannot do much to feed and sustain our essential selves either. Skills are just something which, in that significant modern phrase, we 'take on board', superficially and without full personal commitment.

A particularly telling illustration of the connection between the idea of a 'skill' and our tendency to 'individualize' can be found in the 1995 European White Paper, 'Teaching and Learning: Towards the Learning Society'. We read (pp 2–3) of the aspiration to make the European Union into 'a just and progressive society based on its cultural wealth and diversity…There needs to be permanent and broad access to a number of different forms of knowledge. In addition, the level of skill achieved by each and everyone will have to be converted into **an instrument for measuring individual performance**' (original bold). So we start with the inspiring, communitarian ideal of the just and culturally rich society, but quickly we find that this is based on the atomistic separation of individuals in order to measure and grade them. On p 2, in similar fashion, it is said that the new opportunities require everyone to adapt, 'particularly in assembling one's own qualifications on the basis of "building blocks" of knowledge acquired at different times and in various situations. **The society of the future will therefore be a learning society**' (original bold). The 'learning society', then, appears to be a society where separate, even fragmented, bits of knowledge and skill are assembled by individuals for specific employment purposes. Naturally enough it follows that 'individuals become the principal constructor of their own abilities' (p 14), carrying a 'personal skills card' which allows them 'to have their knowledge and know-how recognised as and when they are acquired' (p 35).

Here, we begin to see, is a great irony. Developments in higher education, in both the UK and continental Europe, are taking place in the name of the learning society, a highly communitarian-sounding thing. Yet *this* kind of learning society turns out to be characterized by a heavy strain of individualism. To point this up by one more example: the UK's Department for Education and Employment (DfEE) maintains a Web site (http://www.lifelonglearning.co.uk/) entitled 'Welcome to UK Lifelong Learning'. Here we read:

> Welcome to the home page of the Individual Learning Division of the Department for Education and Employment (DfEE) – the UK's official Web site for the encouragement, promotion and development of lifelong learning.
> Individual Learning News Issue Four out now!

LEARNING

One outcome of all this – of the strong drive towards individualism, the reduction of diverse kinds of qualities and understanding into 'skills' – is that our conception of learning, the very heart of what, one might think, universities are about – becomes more and more empty and unsatisfactory. Learning is more than a matter of skills. It is more than a matter of knowledge, despite the increasing tendency to talk of 'knowledge management' as a principal task of all complex organizations. It is more than information, despite the reckless way in which some people talk as if university lecturers could be replaced by the Internet and the other trappings of information technology. And it is far too rich and complex to be a function purely of individuals. There are various ways of making this point. One way is to draw out some of the complexities of 'learning together', as we try to do in Chapter 5. The following illustration makes a similar point in a different way.

There is a management training game that takes many forms, but in one variation it goes like this. Four or five teams, of perhaps five or six players, are shown three outline two-dimensional shapes (roughly house-shaped, or cat-shaped, or whatever). Their task will be to fit together smaller pieces – lozenges and big and little triangles and squares – to make up these shapes. They will buy these smaller pieces at one table, called the 'bank', and will be rewarded financially at another, the 'market', when they bring the pieces made up into the shapes which they have seen (and they can go to the 'market' to examine the shapes at any time throughout the game). Once one team has succeeded, the reward for making that particular shape will decrease, and will continue to decrease with each further success. The object of the game is for each team to make as much money as it can. That, pretty well, describes the rules of the game.

The game is intended to show or remind us, vividly in either case, how readily we ignore those aspects of learning which go beyond technical or problem-solving skills. For example, we are often slow to see the importance of building a team, of communication within a team, or of stepping back and looking at our own motivation, assumptions and values. In other words, we have a propensity for looking at tasks in terms of the skills required, neglecting the extent to which successful learning has rich elements of 'learning together' as well as a deep intra-personal dimension. The playing of the game usually shows how much we need to be reminded of these simple points. Players show a strong tendency to see the task as essentially the technical one: how do you get the pieces to fit together to make these awkward shapes? This desire to become immersed in a satisfying technical task often blinds them to the importance of other matters: of checking, for example, that they are not buying pieces at a price which cannot possibly bring them a profit if they succeed (it is easier to make the shapes by using lots of the small triangles, but they are expensive). Often teams will enthusiastically set about trying to solve the puzzle without even checking how much the finished solution will earn them. Often a dominant individual will elect himself (usually it is a he) team leader, holding and manipulating the pieces while others make suggestions. Only rarely do teams hold a meeting first to discuss the task, to allocate roles or to decide to break into subgroups. When they do this, it often becomes very clear that two subgroups are about four times as effective as one large group. When there is preliminary discussion, sometimes it will occur to someone that a good strategy is to see what the other groups are doing, or even to dispatch a member to wait by the 'market' and copy the first successful solution that is brought there (neither strategy has been forbidden in the rules of the game).

Most interesting of all, one of the most common assumptions is that when you have finished one shape the appropriate thing is to go on and try to make the next one. Of course that may not be the right move: the right move may be to repeat the success, as long as you are still being rewarded at a rate that gives you a profit on the pieces you have bought. The pull of the technical, the urge to see if you can solve another puzzle, appears to triumph over all other considerations. In one version of the game the organizer stops the game from time to time and asks the participants to rate their teams on a pro-forma on a number of criteria: how well are they doing on communication, team-building or personal reflection (which might be a matter of asking yourself questions like: am I being self-indulgent? Am I seeking personal success at the expense of the team's? Is there anything here that makes me feel threatened?). Despite this invitation to reflection, it is common to see teams so absorbed in the puzzle that they barely glance at the pro forma. It is also common to see teams, or individuals, obsessed with the idea of stopping other teams' success, for example by trying to buy up all pieces of a certain kind. In fact the game is not competitive – all can make money, without having to do so at each other's expense – and the pricing and availability of the pieces has been designed to frustrate this strategy.

We have not described this game simply in order to give a pen-picture of how learning is more complex than knowledge or information, and how it goes beyond being a function of the individual, though we believe the game does illustrate this well. The example makes a further, and perhaps rather uncomfortable point, which is that some of the richer and more interesting models of human learning available to us come from outside the conventional academic world.

THE ENDS OF HIGHER EDUCATION

Lastly we return to questions of ends, of what higher education is for. Now this is clearly not a technical question, not one which instrumental reason alone can answer. That mode of rationality takes ends as given and enquires into the most efficient way to reach them: here the question is rather how to determine those ends themselves. It is not easy to give a general account of how we determine ends. The current climate, it is probably fair to say, tends to regard our ultimate values either as implanted in us, deterministically, by our genes or upbringing (or both), or as things which we simply choose, opt or plump for. (The influence of genetic research and the philosophy of 'the market' seems easy to trace here.) Thus ends are in part given and in part plucked from the air. To add to the confusion, the hegemony of the market in which the ultimate in free choices are made, so it is supposed, is often treated as itself an unalterable fact of nature. Either way, there appears no room for manoeuvre between what is simply the nature of things on the one hand, and following your nose and your instincts on the other.

However, there are grounds for saying that the picture implicit in popular thinking is a false one. From Aristotle's *Nicomachean Ethics* to a number of sophisticated and convincing modern treatments (eg Larmore, 1987; Dunne, 1993; Richardson, 1997) we find offered the possibility of what many writers have called *rational deliberation*. In rational deliberation about ends there is a complex interplay of reason and emotion, the general and the particular, discursive and non-discursive reasoning. To take an example from Richardson (1997), deciding whether to have children may involve instrumental reasoning, even something like cost-benefit analysis (can we afford to bring up a child in the way we would want to? How would it fit with our other projects and ambitions?). It also involves trying out the idea of having children against one's feelings, and these are complex things that need to be explored in some depth, preferably with the help of someone you trust. Feelings do not, contrary to the popular view, present themselves to us as clear and indubitable. You may have general views about children: that it is irresponsible to bring them into a world like ours, perhaps, or that a marriage or relationship is incomplete without them. You will need to spend some time with real and particular children, in case your general view of them as a class is, one way or another, unrealistic. And a lot of the time we find that we do such deliberation best in the company of others, or that when we reflect in private this often takes the form of an internal argument or dialogue. There is, as Richardson argues (1997: 189), an *embodied* quality to deliberation, 'with passions that influence and integrally express thinking and with perceptual abilities that reflect both trained patterns of thought and commitments to action... Rational deliberation is... not abstractable into a set of relations among propositions'.

Now if this kind of account of rational deliberation is even approximately correct, it is clear that when we deliberate about ends, whether the aims and purposes of higher education, where we are going in our lives, whether to have children or quite what our company or organization stands for, what we are doing involves vastly more than skills and instrumental reason. We need to employ judgement, we need the rudiments of practical wisdom. We need a strong sense of ethics, of what is right as opposed to what is prudential. We need personal visions that we are prepared to explore and perhaps modify, and then commit ourselves to. And we need a rich sense of the diverse particularity of the world, for that supplies us with examples, case studies and tests of our principles. To put it starkly, the narrow sense of learning which pervade the Dearing Report, as so many official publications about education, higher and otherwise, makes rational deliberation impossible. Moreover, rational deliberation requires the rich vein of insight that learning together can provide but which is precluded by the thin individualism which we also find in Dearing. A society formed on Dearing's implicit view of learning could not make sense of itself and its world; the graduates of this kind of higher education could not, simply, understand what higher education was for. They could recall that a degree improves your job prospects, but that is another matter.

In respect of the issues discussed in this chapter, perhaps the kindest thing one can say about the Dearing Report is this: *the more it has to say about the aims, purposes and principles of higher education, the less it could have been written by the kind of people it appears to envisage the universities producing.*

Note

1. For a fuller critique of SCAA's position in this document see Smith and Standish, 1997.

4

The Normalization of Research

Now, perhaps as never before, the question of research is a matter of primary concern for those working in universities. Of course, universities have long been places of research, even if a Newman or, more dramatically, a Jowett[1] might sometimes express doubts about how far research was essential to the institution. What has changed has four key dimensions. First, and most importantly, changes in university funding – above all the reduction in income for students taught – have meant that funding gained through research has assumed greater significance. Second, and related to this, there is the increasingly competitive quasi-market conditions in which universities operate. The research profile of the university is a major factor in its prestige in a world where success builds on success. Third, there is the ending in 1992 of the binary divide between universities and polytechnics, which left the 'traditional' universities anxious to reassert their standing in the field of research and the 'new' universities eager to prove their new credentials. And the fourth concerns a change in the concept of research itself where this has come to be equated with publication.

The new emphasis on research has boosted the already well-established proliferation of journals and conferences, and has enhanced the fortunes of publishing companies now confident of a supply of manuscripts from authors willing to publish for small returns. Within the university it has generated an anxiety and excitement: anxiety where reluctant researchers are pressed to 'produce', where the renewal of contracts is dependent on publication, where departmental fortunes fluctuate with the vicissitudes of external contracts and formalized research ratings; excitement coloured by these same anxieties but aroused by the intrinsic stimulus of the research and by the prospect of the kudos that attaches to success. At the time of the most recent Research Assessment Exercise (RAE), and in the spirit of excitement that

that generated, the leader in the *Times Higher Educational Supplement* could claim:

> The 1996 results show both the level of activity and the quality of research rising. They show a dynamic higher education system which can boast two supremely excellent, large universities – Oxford and Cambridge – locked in a long-running battle for top place, a duel which probably sharpens the performance of both. Alongside Oxford and Cambridge are three other institutions – LSE, Imperial and University College, London which consistently top the league tables at each research assessment with excellent world-class work across the whole range of what they do. And they show a number of general universities, big civics and smaller 1960s foundations, which have a high proportion of their staff – usually more than 80 per cent – engaged in research with little of it rated below grade 3. (*THES*, 20 December 1996: 11)

Perhaps more important, the leader goes on to suggest, is that the system enables growth and improvement, as is shown by the developing and sometimes surprising achievements of new universities. Three probable effects of the availability of the performance data are noted. First, and most obviously, conclusions will be drawn by the market – by prospective students, by funding bodies, by industrial companies in need of research. Second, the information will challenge weaker institutions to improve. Third, on the strength of the information the operation of the market will accelerate the rate of differentiation of institutions. This should be allowed to develop without the interference of central planning: universities are managing themselves well.

This upbeat confidence expressed by the *Times Higher Education Supplement* has not been shared by all. Criticism of the methods of assessment of the research in particular has been legion, and we shall shortly address some of the principal sources of concern. First, however, it is necessary to locate the recommendations for research presented by the Dearing Committee in this new climate. We see the recommendations less as a vision for change than as a product and expression of that climate. So our intention is not to offer detailed criticism of this section of the Report but to suggest that it is more a symptom of, rather than a solution to, the broader problems that climate presents.

At first glance it is difficult to see why anyone should object to the conception of research that governs Dearing's approach to the topic. The specification of aims seems little more than common sense:

- to generate useful knowledge and inventions in support of wealth creation and an improved quality of life;
- to inform and enhance teaching;
- to add to the sum of human knowledge and understanding;
- to create an environment in which researchers can be encouraged and given a high level of training.

For many, the first of these will seem barely controversial at all: surely this is the central reason why the public purse is drawn upon to support research. Others will be quick to point out the way in which the utility of research is placed at the top of the list, and, remembering Newman's fears of the threat from the North (the influence on universities of the booming industries of the North of England), they may argue that such matters are not the proper concern of a university rightly so-called. Against such a view, however, it can be quickly pointed out that this conception of the university has its own form of short-sightedness and is more partial and more recent than is sometimes imagined – witness the role of medieval universities in providing professional training of certain kinds. The university is a changing institution. Appeals to what is essential about the university are less well grounded than some would like to imagine.

The second aim is equally well intentioned even if it is less clear. It may concern two different things. It may refer to the pursuit of pedagogical expertise – an improvement on otherwise leaden lecture delivery, better sensitivity to the different needs of the students of the 'new' higher education, a command of technology sufficient to explore new possibilities of open learning, better communication skills – of which more will be said later. But it may refer to the kind of scholarship within her discipline that an academic engages in. This makes her more knowledgeable in her subject, helping to ensure the authority of her teaching. Perhaps more significant, however, her pursuit of the subject with enthusiasm and sincerity exemplifies the kind of approach that the subject can provoke: students can see her as an embodiment of what the subject is all about. If some of that enthusiasm rubs off on them, this will not be merely useful in motivating them to work hard but internal to what makes the subject worthwhile. This seems to be linked with the third specification, that research should add to the sum of human knowledge and understanding, where there is some inchoate sense that this kind of activity – some of it, at least – is worthwhile in itself. So, for example, having knowledge of history – discovering new things, putting together what we know, reinterpreting the evidence – all this seems to be the kind of activity a civilized society should be prepared to spend (some) money on, and it is right that some people should be supported by the state in such endeavours. Pressed to spell this out or, worse, to defend the claim, it is likely that many would flounder. The idea that something has intrinsic worth frustrates the irremediable drift towards instrumentalism in our justifications of such matters; it frustrates our inclination to look for a return on our investments. Many, nevertheless, may well feel some deference to this not quite understood, even partially mysterious, aspect of university work.

So far so good, we might be inclined to say. But the point is that, so far, much has been left unclear. Should we pass so quickly over questions concerning the nature of research? Should the more or less unexamined common-sense idea of research we have started with (and which Dearing takes as read) be tolerated in precisely the place where assumptions are supposed to be examined – the university? In this light, it should be noticed, the fourth aim of research sits oddly with the rest. Can this really be a distinct *purpose* of research, as opposed to a commitment to provide the conditions that help to stimulate research? This is not just a quibble for it indicates the way in which discussion of the nature and purpose of research is so quickly elided in the Report: attention is turned to questions about means, specifically to how the whole business is to be funded – the sustained focus of the rest of that chapter.

None of this is to deny the very real issues concerning funding that the Report grapples with. Indeed it cannot but be good for the research community that the decline in funding is so publicly recognized. Research in the UK is, we are told, up there with that of the world leaders in terms of both quality and quantity. It is even cost-effective in the use of resources. But the prospects of maintaining this position, when UK expenditure compares unfavourably with our competitors', are not good. Present prestige may rest on past achievements. There is a need to put right past under-investment in the research infrastructure so that the research base is not further eroded. Without this universities will no longer be able to attract funding from industry, nor will they be valued partners with overseas institutions in research. And the nature of the justification for such additional resources is clear: 'The importance of the research base to the national economy, and its cost-effectiveness, provides a strong case for increasing the present level of funding' (Summary, 53). The Report emphasizes, furthermore, that where research is funded it should be adequately funded. Properly supported, it can promote high quality teaching, further applied work, and sustain regional development. Indeed the national interest requires that industry and higher education are brought into stronger partnership in both research and its exploitation for their mutual benefit.

So much good sense then. What can there be against this? And it does seem recurrently in the language of the report that every point of view has been acknowledged and every eventuality covered, such is its comprehensive range and tone. If the aim is 'improved quality of life', this can (within limits) mean what we want it to mean, so the plausibility of the aim is all the harder to resist. The language of the Report sets the limits for debate and clearly marks out the problems that are to be addressed. We shall later in the chapter come to question these limits and to consider problems and tensions that the reforms envisaged by Dearing are unlikely to resolve. First, however, it will be worth saying something about popular perceptions of university research work and considering the bearing these have on the climate in which the recommendations are made. Dearing's audience is not just the universities themselves but includes the wider political constituency with its opinion leaders and vested interests – a constituency, it might be added, well represented on the Committee itself. And rightly so, many will say. Who, after all, is to pay the bill? But this makes the activity of the academy all the more vulnerable to the uncertainties of broader political change, to the prevailing instrumentalism, and to popular images of what research is all about.

A broader frame makes understandable the plausibility of this language. Asked what the research function of a university might be, the average broadsheet reader is likely to think first of medical research. There is not a little self-interest in this response. After all, where is the cure for the cancer that one in four of us are destined to get to come from if not from research, and isn't it the case that much of this goes on in the university? It is evident good sense then that research of *this* kind should be supported. After that the picture may be more hazy. A characteristic of our world is the breathtaking speed of technological innovation. Surely much of the research that brings this about goes on in universities. And yet it is clear that, alongside any collaborative arrangements they may engage in with universities, major industries make huge investments in their own R&D (research and development). In its complementary and leading roles then, the university's research function must be tied to technological progress. The history of science is indeed one of progress, faltering at times perhaps but making up for this with leaps and bounds of success, its knowledge steadily accumulating. There is no end to the ills that science can address nor any doubt about the unforeseen improvements to life that it will otherwise bring. In the dying years of the twentieth century, however, few will entertain these thoughts without a disturbing awareness of the harm that industrial innovation and advance also bring. It is all too obvious that changes bringing increased human comfort and the wider availability of material goods are often at the same time threats to the environment, sometimes constituting threats to the planet that far outweigh any benefits they could possibly bring. If this qualifies faith in technological innovation, it does not substantially weaken it: to clear up the mess that has been created, and, to avoid such problems in the future, what do we need but a refined and more sensitively attuned technology?

Of course, the university's range of research is broader than examples from science and technology might suggest and this will be evident too. So, let's assume, there is some recognition that the pundits called upon by *Newsnight* to discuss foreign policy or housing benefit or the laws of privacy are better informed precisely as a result of their engagement in disinterested research into these matters. It may further be recognized that such research is not undertaken by isolated individuals but depends on some kind of research community – not the culturally broad collegial milieu that an earlier age of university dons drew upon, and flourished (or languished) in, but a combination of colleagues involving some of the academic's department and extending through those networks of relationship sustained in conferences, journals, and other academic writing. This is the age of specialization and we need new techniques to address problems in all spheres. With the knowledge explosion and the proliferation we need experts to make sense of it all.

More generally there may well be some vague sense that those who are teaching in universities should be, if not at the cutting edge of their disciplines, at least *au fait* with the kinds of debates that are the current focuses of research. It is part of the common perception that one can expect something of university lecturers here that one cannot reasonably ask of lecturers in further education or of schoolteachers – this is higher education after all. How else in any case can their relatively light teaching load and long holidays be justified? Moreover it may be that our broadsheet reader has memories of lecturers who inspired, and who were inspiring not just because they were driven to pursue their subject beyond the demands of the immediate course material but because they somehow or other connected with the august names on the reading lists.

The broad thrust of these remarks, however, is to the effect that hackneyed images of Ivory Tower irrelevance have been displaced by something newer. In an age of technique, expertise acquires a new style, and academic research has the potential to seem altogether more sexy. There may also be a degree of suspicion and perhaps of envy of the international conference-hopping that has seemed – for some, at least – to go with it:

> It's June, and the conference season is well and truly open. In Oxford and Rummidge, to be sure, the students still sit at their desks in the examination halls, like prisoners in the stocks, but their teachers are able to flit off for a few days before the scripts come in for marking; while in North America the second semester of the academic year is already finished, papers have been graded, credits awarded, and the faculty are free to collect their travel grants and head east, or west, or wherever their fancy takes them. *Wheeeeeeeeee!*
>
> The whole academic world seems to be on the move. Half the passengers on transatlantic flights these days are university teachers. Their luggage is heavier than average, weighed down with books and papers – and bulkier, because their wardrobes must embrace both formal wear and leisurewear, clothes for attending lectures in and clothes for going to the beach in, or to the Museum, or the Schloss, or the Duomo, or the Folk Village. For that's the attraction of the conference circuit: it's a way of converting work into play, combining professionalism with tourism, and all at someone else's expense. Write a paper and see the world! I'm Jane Austen – fly me! Or Shakespeare, or T. S. Eliot, or Hazlitt. All tickets to ride, to ride the jumbo jets. *Wheeeeeeeeee!*
> (Lodge, 1993: 465–6)

On the conference circuit life barely touches the ground, it seems. What these academics lack in terms of connectedness with everyday practical affairs they make up in style, and style is technique. The Ivory Tower Scholar has been replaced in the popular imagination by something closer to the High Flyer. Such images in novels or on television are powerful influences on popular perceptions. If the hint of celebrity and success in at least some of the lives so depicted arouses a degree of envy, it does this in virtue of the kudos that attaches to research (popularly glamorized perhaps with the increasingly common American stress on the first syllable). It is, is it not, the élite activity of the university?

If these expectations reflect a kind of common sense, it is common sense also that has shaped the conclusions about the nature and point of research that Dearing takes as its starting point. On closer scrutiny too many will feel that the conception of research stands up well. But there is a vacuity in the world that Lodge depicts, now 20 years old, that has its echoes in the research climate of more recent years. Is this the life of the academic today? That such experience may be true of a minority only of university staff is not really the point. The vacuity has come to take new forms and not a little of the glamour has worn off.

The anxiety generated by the RAE is not something that operates at a purely individual level. Research assessment is not of individuals but of departments, and grants are commonly awarded to research teams. The criteria for such grants and the ratings conferred become, for some, something of an obsession. Staff are brought together in a shared anxiety about how to improve the department's performance, and this is formalized through research committees and systems for monitoring performance. These practices generate their own new orthodoxy. Research is to be managed and focused, with staff researching in collaborative clusters. For optimum results, all academic staff in a department should be 'research-active'. (If they are not someone should make sure that the inactive are not entered in the next RAE – above all, make sure that any tail of weak researchers is cut off.) In the harsher contemporary world of competition for scarce resources, the story goes, these are difficult tasks, and it becomes evident that size matters: it is necessary to maintain a department with sufficient critical mass to support an appropriate range of research activity. The collegial and democratic organization of universities in fact makes this all the more realizable as larger departments will be able to vote in their own interests, maintaining their size and consolidating their position. And there is an intuitive plausibility to this, difficult though it is to disentangle the principle from the kind of rationalization that vested interests and the operations of university politics could well engender. Yet a variety of studies have called into question the popular assumption that large departments are more productive (cp Cave *et al*, 1997: 175–6). True, there is a threshold below which support for research is inadequate, but it seems that beyond this there is no significant gain and that economies of scale are often negated by human factors. The impression that can be given by big departments of being hives of research activity is a misleading one.

'Appropriate range' need not involve the department in the comprehensive coverage of all fields of the discipline but it must show a spread of expertise and activity over at least some of its central areas. It has become something of a cliché that competition between departments has encouraged football-style scouting for top researchers with a rush to sign people up before the cut-off point for eligibility for the RAE, a destabilizing factor in university research which the next exercise is surely to address. In the wake of these star signings there is a trail of short-term appointments – fixed-term lecturers and research assistants earnestly 'producing' to merit extensions to contracts. This casualization of employment creates a level of insecurity that can hardly be conducive to the reflection and imagination on which good research so heavily depends. It puts a premium on the appearance of activity and encourages 'presenteeism'. (Dr Piercemuller checks his pigeon-hole four times an hour![2]) It also encourages pretence. It becomes more important that research papers are published than that they arise from authentic commitment. For all the emphasis on the strategic management of research it encourages short-term planning and the adoption of 'safe' research projects which can be completed on time, whose findings are acceptable to their sponsors, and which can be published in time for the next RAE. To make this possible inordinate amounts of time are spent by researchers not on academic work but in applying for research funding. The provision of advice on how to go about this is becoming a mini-industry in itself within universities. Some staff complain that they spend more time doing this than reading books! The gaining of research contracts is also made more urgent by the fact that jobs may depend on it: for research assistants this is crucial and many lecturing staff feel driven to secure contracts in order to keep research assistants in work. The combined effect of these anxieties is to create a research culture quite different from that comically exemplified by the High Flyers. The busyness of research assistants anxious to earn an extension of their contracts, the frenetic activity of academic staff, the processing of data – this is the research culture of the Shop Floor.

A threat that faces many departments (and universities) is that research will be concentrated in centres of excellence, and indeed it is likely that, beyond the already apparent effects of the market, national policy will soon institutionalize such a differentiation. For those excluded this spells more teaching, less money for conferences, less incentive to research, less prestige – and an unseemly scramble for places in élite departments and institutions. Such a concentration of resources will depend on the results of assessment and hence the mechanisms of this have all the more impact on the ethos of the Shop Floor.

In certain respects the competition these changes have generated is highly beneficial. Of course, those engaged in research have long been motivated by the kind of competitive impulse that arises from the desire to 'be there' first or to write the ground-breaking paper. To some extent personal satisfaction and institutional prestige have turned on such matters. What is new is the way that quantified assessment has led to formal rankings and to the mentality of league tables. Assessment of research is in a sense unavoidable and is indeed something academics would not want to be without. Once research comes into the public domain it is important to the researchers themselves that it is considered and evaluated. How else is its value to be recognized? What is not inevitable, however natural this may have come to seem, is that assessment must be quantified. Thus it is the nature of measurement that requires consideration, for it is arguable that this has not only led to cynical manoeuvrings to gain results – encouraged, it might be added, by the sometimes spurious criteria – but also had a bearing on the ethical context in which academic work is undertaken. Human beings are not slow to display petty vices, and academics are no exception. When the results of the last RAE were released Laurie Taylor aptly highlighted the meanness of spirit that sometimes takes the place of the disinterested pursuit of truth: "'Well done, old chap, I see your department picked up a 4." "Oh yes." "Shouldn't you be pleased? It's an excellent ranking. Only one down from our 5.'" (THES, 20 December 1996) As we shall see below, however, what is at stake in terms of the ethical framework for research goes well beyond this kind of human frailty.

What can be said about the measurement of performance in the RAE? To begin with it must be acknowledged that the basis of the method in peer review is strongly to be supported. The system is much valued by academics, and alternatives are fraught with problems. Fellow researchers are the most significant constituency in the public domain, however much this can be compromised by the need to appeal to funding bodies or other sponsors. But who is a peer? This question arises first in virtue of the broad subject categorizations within which research must be entered. How can comparatively small assessment panels be sufficiently familiar with work in all the fields that they must assess? Research that goes beyond what they know, especially where it breaks with conventional approaches, may simply not be recognizable. A related problem concerns the selection of panels. The need to ensure a reasonable coverage of the range of a subject exerts a conservative influence that is likely to reinforce central areas of the disciplines. Something of this conservatism is recognized by Dearing: the RAE tends to favour those who work in central areas of a discipline, and the need to redress this through mechanisms to promote joint and collaborative activities by institutions and interdisciplinary work is emphasized. There is, furthermore, the problem of the existence of rival paradigms in a discipline, rivalries sometimes characterized by incomprehension if not hostility. This makes all the more equivocal the role of panel members and may undermine the search for common criteria across the broad range of a subject, regardless of alternative traditions and paradigms. It is sometimes claimed that the assessment of research suffers from a lack of clear criteria. The danger of explicitness, however, is that it could exacerbate these problems.

While the practice of peer review is strongly supported by the academic community, the use of performance indicators, and especially of bibliometric means of assessment, is viewed with understandable misgivings. There is unease about the way that performance indicators that generally have been devised for the pure and applied sciences are being used in the humanities and social sciences. These practices can obscure other ways in which meaningful research can take place, ways that the idea of scholarship seems to encapsulate. Thus it is sometimes suggested that, whereas research in the sciences typically involves finding out something new, scholarship requires the reconsideration and interpretation of what is already known (Cave *et al*, 1997: 165). Whether this is an adequate differentiation will become clearer towards the end of this chapter.

With regard to the use of citation indexes, problems with bias and distortion are of four main kinds. First, where an idea becomes firmly established, its originator may not be given due credit, and subsequent commentators may be referred to instead. Second, a ground-breaking paper may not be understood, breaking as it does with received ideas and perhaps with orthodox practices. Third, there is the problem of self-citation. Fourth, there is negative citation, where reference is made to a work that is believed to be profoundly wrong, even bad. (Thus, Jensen's paper on racial superiority is one of the most cited social science papers.) Finally there is the problem of in-group and deferential citations where authors reciprocally admire each other's work or perhaps flatter institutionally influential players in the field. (For a fuller discussion see Cave *et al*, 170, 184–6.)

A further factor regarding competition has to do with the prowess of British institutions in the international arena. It is likely that the credibility of the RAE from an international perspective will be enhanced by international representation on assessment panels, and this is very likely to be beneficial in terms of the safeguarding of standards. Comparison with the research performance of other countries in similar economic circumstances is motivated by a competition for prestige but it is also a competition for the financial rewards that go with prestige, often linked directly to commercial income. It cannot be denied that this competition stimulates research activity and enterprise and, in many respects, a healthy international research culture. But the competitive emphasis can lead also to a conception of the point of research in relative terms rather than in the absolute terms of the pursuit of truth ('unrealistic' though this kind of assertion has inevitably come to sound).

There are clearly big stakes to play for here and hence a possible reinforcement of the subjugation of research to the needs of the economy. A common complaint concerning the last RAE, one endorsed by Dearing, is that the system does not sufficiently reward applied research. In part this was voiced by the new universities who could claim that the system failed adequately to acknowledge their strengths precisely because these were in applied fields. This may be a valid point but the promotion of the applied has the potential to colonize the very conception of research, strongly supported as this is by what many lay people imagine research to be about, as we saw at the start of this chapter. Ironically a concentration on applied research seems to fail even in its own terms: when research in the Soviet Union was confined to the applied, it soon fell behind. Furthermore any shift towards applied research in universities makes equivocal the relationship with industry. Industry conducts much of its own R&D so the role that the universities have becomes less distinctive and less clear.

We drew attention above to the way that the fourth aim of research specified by the Dearing Report is scarcely an aim *of research* at all. Rather it concerns the way in which an appropriate research culture can be developed, in particular through the training of young researchers. Broadly endorsing the 'Review of postgraduate education' chaired by Professor Martin Harris, the Report makes the following recommendations:

> The requirements of research training include an understanding of a range of research methods, and competence in relevant technical skills, as well as the development of relevant professional skills. For industry – and other forms of employment – professional skills include the ability to operate effectively in a commercial environment, to be able to communicate ideas in writing and orally to a variety of audiences, to work effectively in teams as well as independently, and to develop high level planning and self-management skills. (para. 11.84)

This is, is it not, preparation for the Shop Floor? We shall not dwell on the shift in the paragraph to the context of industry. What is more significant is the vocabulary of efficiency and effectiveness: 'technical skills', 'professional skills', 'operate effectively', 'work effectively', 'planning and self-management skills'. Even the word 'communicate' might imply that language itself has become another skill. And the suggestion that training should prepare researchers for both teamwork (where complementary capabilities are brought together, and where it is assumed that there is a common understanding of what the 'problem' is and only difference in the techniques used for analysing it) and independent work (where others are not needed) seems sufficiently comprehensive to finesse any idea that research might crucially involve something more like dialogue.

Having hinted at the limitations here let us pass on to a broader question concerning the concept of a research culture itself. We have used this now common phrase in this chapter but it remains to be asked what exactly 'culture' means here. Current usage in this context suggests not so much high culture as yeast. The research culture then is understood in a way that could be argued to be helpfully organic but the underlying assumption is that a research community can be created, or at least promoted, through the application of certain techniques. There is some truth to this and it would be quite wrong to lose sight of the various practical measures that are necessary if research is to be encouraged. Nor would it be right to underestimate the importance of such general skills as are relevant to at least some types of research and to fail to train people in these. The problem with this idea of a research culture is the way it deflects attention from the deeper and less easily identified commitments and relationships that are intrinsic to a healthy research climate. It redefines the landscape of research in a way that is potentially stultifying. To expand on the nature of this we need to review another of the aims that Dearing specifies.

It is presented as uncontroversial that research should 'add to the sum of human knowledge and understanding', and the assumption tacitly underwrites the kind of approach that is taken to be appropriate in research training. Of course, the phrase has a lofty ring to it and, again, one might wonder why anyone should object. But the phrase 'add to the sum' betrays an incrementalism that needs to be challenged. At its crudest this is the bucket theory of knowledge. It takes for granted an empirical scientific model and loses sight not only of the variety of disciplines but of the variety within any one discipline. Indeed if this variety is to be appreciated it should be recognized that research will be better understood if assumptions about what is essential to it are relinquished in favour of acceptance of its non-systematic diversity. Research activities are related in the way of family resemblance, with endless overlapping and connecting features but with no characteristic common to all.

What is more, the picture we are presented with gets science wrong. It trades on the popular misconception of the scientist as someone who gathers data and thereby discovers things, totally underestimating the nature and the role of theory formation (without which it is not even clear that data collection makes sense). It imagines the scientist to be someone who systematically pursues an idea along the railway tracks of methodical organization. Normal research goes on, it is true, but someone in a corner is doing something wacky and succeeding where others encounter only a problem. In his review of James Watson's personal account of the discovery of the structure of DNA, Peter Medawar uncovers the mistake with admirable conciseness:

> A good many people will read *The Double Helix* for the insight they hope it will bring them into the nature of the creative process in science. It may indeed become a standard case history of the so-called 'hypothetico-deductive' method at work. Hypothesis and inference, feedback and modified hypothesis, the rapid alternation of imaginative and critical episodes of thought – here it can all be seen in motion, and every scientist will see that same intellectual structure in the research he does himself. It is characteristic of science at every level, and indeed of most exploratory or investigative approaches in everyday life. No layman who reads this book with any kind of understanding will ever again think of the scientist as a man who cranks a machine of discovery. No beginner in science will henceforward believe that discovery is bound to come his way if he practices a certain Method, goes through a certain well-defined performance of hand and mind. (Medawar in Watson, 1981: 224)

If the incrementalism of Dearing's terminology is inappropriate to this kind of science, the idea that research might 'generate useful knowledge' in the first recommendation smacks of a kind of factory production – the cranking out of new facts and inventions – that is similarly inappropriate to technology. Above all what is missing here is a sense of the importance of the imagination. And this deficit is scarcely redressed where contemporary research is theorized in terms of knowledge production, for this in its turn borrows support from a fashionable version of social constructivism that inadvertently reinforces the Shop Floor ethos, whatever sceptical or relativistic commitments it may bring in its train. It is not that the Shop Floor ethos is wholly inappropriate; indeed this is just how much research takes place today. What is wrong is the way its practices have come to spread throughout the organization of research and to colonize thinking in fields where it is inappropriate.

The oddly inert and apparently value-free word 'data', covering over any richer sense of *what is given*, is apt to convey a rigour that displaces any sense of the way that tentative exploration, criticism, and with luck inspiration figure in scientific work. 'Information', no less, conveys a picture of bits and pieces of facts lying about and waiting to be picked up. It goes without saying that we then need the skills of accessing and processing that enable us to pile up knowledge in ways that are useful. Information technology itself, as we argue in Chapter 7, constantly reinforces the incremental picture, in the process informing the researchers themselves – channelling their very thinking. This apparent neutrality can cover over the fact that much knowledge is not what it is cracked up to be: theories are superseded, not all facts are important. Spurious notions of objective rigour can hide the fact that good research can change what counts. Let us not forget also that if research is to inform and enhance teaching, the Report's second aim for research, teaching itself will become skewed in this way.

If we recall the various ways in which there are conservative pressures on research, if we acknowledge the interaction of new systems of accountability and performance assessment (with their inherent tendency to impose uniformity), if we recognize the way funding bodies allocate awards, we can see how the incrementalism of the Shop Floor ethos is supported. The effects of these measures are not to be understood in terms of the malign intervention of the state, though sometimes this description may have seemed just. There is a curtailment of freedom here, though not primarily to do with academic freedom as this has commonly been understood. It is brought about by the 'soft despotism' of management, to borrow de Tocqueville's phrase. Freedom is curtailed through normalization. Dearing's neutrality contributes to the normalizing tendencies that are now so strongly present and which manifest themselves in the current research climate.

It was said earlier that the idea of research tends to be dominated by an empirical scientific model. The history of science has special significance then as a model of knowledge for the academy at this time. However much a debased popular understanding of science may adversely affect the conceptualization and practice of research, there is a deeper problem to do with science's way of understanding itself: science tends to rewrite its own history in terms of ever more encompassing standpoints, with a view to ever more comprehensive explanation. It is arguable that this practice seems more natural than it is, and that this naturalness is underpinned by the exclusion of viewpoints that do not fit easily into the prevailing view. It is evident that the science curriculum varies comparatively little from one country to another. Perhaps it is significant that this does not cause us great surprise. But is our very lack of surprise a measure of the normalization and standardization that science is thereby effecting?

A further aspect of this normalization has to do with the way that a technological approach is increasingly evident, in those systems of quality control that universities are increasingly borrowing from further education. It is a feature of technology that it has the capacity to displace other ways of thinking and thus to extend into areas where it is not appropriate.

Having established that normalization is a central problem for research it is time to turn attention to the kinds of research communities that are needed if a fruitful research culture is to be created. What are the required conditions? How are these patterns of normalization most constructively disturbed? And how is the frenetic activity of the Shop Floor ethos to be replaced by modes of organization more conducive to enquiry? Faith in the research potential of the independent researcher or of the collaborative team needs to be replaced by a more sound account of the kind of community on which research must rely. One thing to be acknowledged initially is that there are limits to the extent to which a community can be wilfully created. Planning, as we have seen, is apt to exert conservative influence and ultimately to stultify the kind of growth that is essential to fruitful research. At a more mundane level the idea of planning a community ignores the fact that people will meet who they meet: successful collaborations often arise fortuitously and spontaneously. They share with friendship a resistance to planning.

Of course the community need not be a community made up of persons now present. Inasmuch as research is an aspect of academic subjects it constitutes a part of the conversation of mankind, in Michael Oakeshott's phrase. Even the most solitary research involves a partnership between the living, the dead, and the as yet unborn. And, contrary to the current vogue for research collaboration, it may well be that this conversation is best pursued by people in solitude. As Emerson puts it, solitude may be necessary to become acquainted with one's thoughts:

> In this distribution of functions the scholar is the delegated intellect. In the right state he is *Man Thinking*. In the degenerate state, when the

victim of society, he tends to become a mere thinker, or still worse, the parrot of other men's thinking. In this view of him, as Man Thinking, the theory of his office is contained. Him Nature solicits with all her placid, all her monitory pictures; him the past instructs; him the future invites. Is not indeed every man a student, and do not all things exist for the student's behoof? And, finally, is not the true scholar the only true master? But the old oracle said, 'All things have two handles: beware of the wrong one.' In life, too often, the scholar errs with mankind and forfeits his privilege. Let us see him in his school, and consider him in reference to the main influence he receives... (Emerson, 1985: 85)

The 'delegated intellect' has its counterpart in the 'neutral stance' that has been criticized above. A picture of mercenary specialists and research technicians comes to colonize our imaginings of what research might be so that the Man Thinking disappears from the picture. This is an impoverishment of learning that carries with it a diminution of the person. In Eugene Kamenka's words, the individual becomes abstract:

> The abstract individual, who is nothing, is elevated against everything that stands outside him; the alleged requirements of the present and the future are counterposed, uncritically, against everything that has come before. For such a view of the world, the past is a lifeless museum, a random collection of bric-a-brac, a storehouse from which we draw items at will, abstracting them from their social and historical context and from the particular kinds of men, women, traditions and institutions that created them. This technique has impoverished our lives and our culture while it appears, superficially, to enrich them...We have become *actors* in the sense that the word had for the Romans – people capable of assuming the *externals* of *any personality* because they have none of their own. (Kamenka, 1980: 18–19)

How alien this language sounds, and not merely because of the rhythms of Emerson's nineteenth-century prose or because of Kamenka's classical allusions! These words will perhaps sound irremediably high-minded or lofty or, put plainly, unrealistic. Not that Dearing is entirely deaf to such words. On the contrary, the Report is peppered with references to the disinterested pursuit of truth or, in more anodyne language, to pure research. Dearing is not deaf to these words but benignly tolerant, which amounts wittingly or unwittingly to a form of tokenism, and this is explained by the earnest commitment to make the Report comprehensive, properly to include the range of informed opinion. But the effect of this is as of an inoculation: pure research has been acknowledged, so who can complain? Sources of dissent that might otherwise have contributed to a more fertile consideration of the questions at hand have thereby been 'taken out'. Alasdair MacIntyre puts this forcefully:

> Academic organisational forms can on occasion effectively exclude from academic debate and enquiry points of view insufficiently assimilable by the academic *status quo*, and they characteristically achieve this exclusion not by formally placing the excluded doctrine under a ban or a prohibition, but by admitting it only in reduced or distorted versions, so that it unavoidably becomes an ineffective contender for intellectual and moral allegiance. (MacIntyre, 1990: 219)

Even to entertain these thoughts requires us to attend to a language different from that of contemporary reports or for that matter from much academic writing on higher education. Pursuing the enquiry into conditions that promote a research culture will require us to go further down this road.

It was said above that the normalizing tendencies in the current research climate constitute a curtailment of freedom. Academic freedom requires something more than the liberty to publish. Processes of normalization subdue the development of those very ideas that would extend research. It is not just that there is pressure to meet the needs of industry – indeed, as we argue in Chapter 6, this is often beneficial; it is that normalization leads to an entrenchment of received opinion, where genuine originality is likely to be replaced by faddishness or modishness. Freedom to think and the possibility of thinking well are fatefully weakened by the tranquilizing terms of 'focused', 'clustered', and above all 'managed' research and the deadening machinery of grant applications. At the same time the very easiness of the production of some research brings its own self-deception. These factors block the kind of thinking that Emerson evokes and frustrate the conversation of mankind.

Normalization – connecting as it does with incrementalism and the stance of neutrality – goes hand in hand with a kind of nihilism. Alasdair MacIntyre's account of the development of the Enlightenment values into the epistemology of encyclopaedism of the liberal university lays bare the limitations of neutrality and of a disinterested rationality where this is not grounded in the moral framework of a particular tradition. The legacy of this is the kind of moral vacuum that universities have found themselves in in the late twentieth century, at a time when established notions of the institution, no less than the foundationalist thinking that once underpinned its epistemology, have been irrevocably undermined. Into this vacuum has come the language of efficiency and effectiveness and the kind of fatuous affirmations of purpose that mission statements so easily become. Meanwhile the expression of the characteristic academic purpose of the university has been subdued:

> For when a number of very different external critics of the university – some deeply hostile, some not hostile but still deeply critical – have proposed from outside the universities measures by which the achievements of contemporary universities should be evaluated and in accordance with which from now on resources should be allocated to them, the official spokespersons of the academic *status quo* have with rare exceptions responded with stuttering ineptitudes. (MacIntyre, 1990: 221)

This reticence scarcely protects the universities in their role of safeguarding freedom. Limiting influences on the research of the university through normalization combine with a new sense of the legitimacy of its direction from outside. Returning to the question of the purpose of universities, MacIntyre writes:

> The beginning of any worthwhile answers to such questions, posed by some external critic, as 'What are universities for?' or 'What peculiar goods do universities serve?' should be, 'They are, when they are true to their own vocation, institutions within which the form "What are x's for?" and "What peculiar goods do y's serve?" are formulated and answered in the best rationally defensible way.' That is to say, when it is demanded of a university community that it justify itself by specifying what its peculiar or essential function is, that function which, were it not to exist, no other institution could discharge, the response of the community ought to be that universities are places where conceptions of and standards of rational justification are elaborated, put to work in the detailed practices of enquiry, and themselves rationally evaluated, so that only from the university can the wider society learn how to conduct its own debates, practical or theoretical, in a rationally defensible way. (MacIntyre, 1990: 222)

Such an endeavour, MacIntyre argues, is only possible where the university makes possible the conduct of intellectual and moral warfare between rival and antagonistic views. Of course there is debate within particular frameworks for thought and this is the stuff of everyday academic activity but it is the larger dialectic between frameworks of thinking that, in MacIntyre's view, is lacking:

> It is precisely because universities have not been such places and have in fact organised enquiry through institutions and genres well designed to prevent them and to protect them from being such places that the official responses of both the appointed leaders and the working members of university communities to their recent external critics have been so lamentable. (MacIntyre, 1990: 222)

The large-scale questions about the purpose of the university, like many other large-scale questions with which they are intertwined, should be taken as questions to which the answers are not straightforward and over which one must struggle but the asking of which is not futile. Yet it is one or other of these assumptions and sometimes both that tend to characterize the running of the modern university. In the preliberal university, according to MacIntyre, there was a homogeneity of fundamental belief which supported and determined what was to count as standards of rational justification. Standards were maintained and strengthened through the process of enquiry itself, through the exclusion from the university of certain groups, subjects, and practices, and through the promotion of those staff who most clearly maintained those standards. While this measure of orthodoxy was enabling, it also was the cause of considerable injustice (in some of its exclusions); ultimately also its conservative tendencies had within them the seeds of a gradual debilitation. The liberal university was alert to the injustices of its predecessor but made the false assumption that practices that sought to ensure the sustaining of common fundamental beliefs amongst its members could be abandoned in favour of a reliance on the standards of rationality unconstrained by any religious or moral beliefs that its members held in common. Yet the outstanding rise of science in the liberal university has not been achieved without its own largely unnoticed exclusions. More generally, agreement on technique has often substituted for agreement on matters of substance. Technical approaches have proliferated across the humanities and social sciences, often being adopted in areas to which they are not suited, the alternative to this being imagined to be limitless absence of agreement. The apparent tolerance of such a liberal institution reduces to something more like indifference, which paradoxically must then reject and marginalize those intolerant positions of constrained religious and moral belief which characterized the preliberal university. The assumption that resolution of these disagreements is required in order that rational enquiry can proceed means that those propounding irreconcilable points of view must be marginalized or otherwise excluded. It is a persistent feature of contemporary debate, and typical of Dearing, that the kinds of question MacIntyre imagines being addressed to the university are dealt with in peremptory fashion and then airily passed by to get on with the real business of the Committee's work – the business of funding. The real challenge to the university is reflected in the fact that the liberal institution, where rationality is thought to provide the sufficient and morally neutral grounds for the maintenance of standards and the pursuit of enquiry, has created a vacuum and an impoverishment. Crucially this failure is now entrenched in a system which in its subservience to the criteria of technical efficiency – understood especially in terms of cost-effectiveness – has so shored itself up against other points of view that these seem Utopian or nostalgic or unacceptably partisan. And it has shored itself up in such a way as to make these values (of cost-effectiveness and efficiency) seem natural, and to render any opposition to them 'unrealistic'.

What is needed is the pursuit of research in such a way that it persists within a tradition but where it at the same time exposes itself to other rival systematic ways of pursuing the subject of its research. Sustaining rival traditions, each critical and dialogic, is a necessary condition for a vibrant research ethos, one that avoids the pitfalls of Ivory Tower, High Flyers, and Shop Floor. Sustaining rival traditions is a condition of freedom.

Notes

1. Jaroslav Pelikan quotes the following words from Newman: 'The view taken of a University in these Discourses is the following: – That it is a place of teaching universal knowledge. This implies that its object is, on the one hand, intellectual, not moral; and, on the other, that it is the diffusion and extension of knowledge rather than *the advancement [of knowledge]*. If its object were scientific and philosophical discovery, I do not see why a University should have students; if religious training, I do not see how it can be the seat of literature and science.' He goes on to quote the remark attributed to Benjamin Jowett by Logan Pearsall Smith: 'Research!... A mere excuse for idleness; it has never achieved , and will never achieve, any results of the slightest value'. (Pelikan, 1992: 78; 85)
2. In Laurie Taylor's weekly column in the *Times Higher Education Supplement*.

5

Learning Together

This chapter is about the kind of teaching and learning that go on in the university, and how they might be made better. 'Made better': this is a colourless expression, but we use it deliberately. Any more vigorous form of words immediately begs questions, and this is itself the first point to note about conceptions of teaching and learning, both in general and as they apply to higher education. For example, it is very common now to see good teaching and learning described in terms of 'effectiveness'. In primary and secondary education this has led to a massive 'effective schools' movement, both in this country and elsewhere (see, for example, Reynolds and Teddlie, 1997). Dearing, for its part, notes that the Committee's terms of reference say that 'the effectiveness of teaching and learning should be enhanced' (8.4). Talk of effectiveness however is not as neutral as it may seem to be. As one of the key terms of technical or instrumental reason (see below, and also Chapter 3) it immediately takes us in the direction of ideas of delivering a curriculum, of the management of learning, and of appropriate strategies for management (cp Dearing 8.15: 'an effective strategy will involve guiding and enabling students to be effective learners, to understand their own learning styles, and to manage their own learning' – note the circularity: effective strategies lead to effective learning). The assumptions here – which are precisely assumptions about the hegemony of technical or instrumental reason – can be challenged. They encourage us to *technicize* higher education, as if whatever needs doing can be brought about by adjusting a system, adding a module, or introducing discrete new skills and techniques, the tools of instrumentality.

So widespread has this way of talking and thinking become, so much has it come to seem the natural and only way to talk about teaching and learning in the university – the default language, one might say – that anyone who wishes to avoid falling into it needs to adopt a deliberate strategy. The strategy we use here is that of talking about the *relationships* between university teachers and students. We start with some very untechnical and unscientific remarks about what students seem to value in their teachers, and with three sketches of what we hope are recognizable types of lecturers. Then we continue discussion under the headings first of 'ethics' and then of 'democracy', dimensions of learning which resist technicist assumptions by continually reminding us of three important things. They remind us that learning has a communal and not purely individual function, that we need constantly to enquire what its *purpose* is, and that, in a sense that will be explained, certain kinds of learning have 'internal goods' that demand respect and must not be neglected in the quest for 'learning outcomes' – the drive for effective universities, departments and lecturers. At the end of the chapter we consider one particular question about the purpose of higher education and its connection with the economy. We acknowledge the legitimate relationship between higher education and the needs of industry and commerce, and consider how these needs appear in the light of the rest of the chapter.

STUDENTS AND LECTURERS

What do students value in the university lecturers who teach them? What follows derives from what some students in the universities in which we work – quite possibly unrepresentatively, certainly with no pretence here of a 'scientific' survey – have told us, not just recently as we began to think about the post-Dearing university, but over many years. The reader may or may not find that it accords with his or her own intuitions and experience.

The central idea that emerged repeatedly and unmistakably from these discussions was that of 'approachability'. The good lecturer, it appears, is open, accessible, thinks about what you have said before responding to you. There is an open relationship, 'one where you don't think, well, he's the lecturer and I'm the student'. The approachable lecturer is someone whom you can, quite literally, go up and talk to. One student illustrated this partly by contrast:

> My mother is a mature student at ——, and right at the beginning they were told, 'your lecturers are important people, they have research to do, you don't go up to them in the street and talk to them'. Here Professor —— says hello when I bump into him in Marks and Spencer, he knows my name. It sounds silly but that means a lot.

When asked to describe this composite approachable lecturer a little further, students said, without hesitation, 'someone who takes an interest in you', 'willing to help', 'you need that personal contact'. At the same time they were clear that this has to be accompanied by enthusiasm, even 'passion', for the subject. 'Otherwise', observed one discussant, 'it's not clear what you would be approaching them about, if you see what I mean'.

These were not the only points made. There was some comment that the good lecturer was knowledgeable, interesting, well-organized and clear in expression. But these points were made in the spirit: 'of course, you should be able to take that for granted. That's not the really important thing'. What emerged clearly, and what we have tried to bring out in the summary above, was the emphasis on a certain kind of *personal relationship*.

What, meanwhile, of the lecturers? Lecturer A senses (perhaps he has nothing as fully worked-out as a theory) that his students stand to learn from him as an enquirer rather than a source of knowledge. He therefore allows himself to stray while teaching into those areas of his subject which seem to him currently most worth inquiring into, even if these are areas where he is unsure what the questions, let alone the answers, are. This has the consequence that parts of his lectures sometimes take the form 'this is puzzling, even baffling' rather than 'this is what is known, and here it is lucidly set out for you'. He defends this, and sometimes has to do so against those students who prefer a lecture which gives them 'a clear set of notes' ('We'd like more overhead transparencies with bullet-points'), on the grounds that he is being true to the nature of his subject, which does not lend itself to simple summaries and solutions. If he were less modest he might add that students stand to gain by his example: he appears to them as one practising his subject rather than as one presenting the results of others' practice and research. If he knew more of the history of philosophy he might mention the pedagogical value of *aporia*, of allowing the student to follow (often commonsensical) assumptions into a kind of mire or *impasse* from which there is no easy route out. His course evaluations tend to be mixed, with students polarized between the highly enthusiastic and the puzzled and slightly resentful. They include complaints of 'not always knowing where we were'.

Lecturer B, even in these days of overwhelming student numbers, persists in trying to remember students' names. At the beginning of the course she plays ice-breaking games to encourage students to learn each others' names too. The walls of her office are covered with sheets of card bearing photographs and names; she refreshes herself from these before each seminar and tutorial. She works hard at showing the relevance of her subject, social anthropology, to her students' lives. First-years are required to consider the bizarre rituals of Faculty registration as an anthropological phenomenon, perhaps a *rite de passage* ('We've looked at how it came to be historically. Now let's see what it might *mean*'); Durkheim provides an opportunity for them to see that other features of student life, such as loneliness and depression, may be functions of social organization and not something which, mysteriously and perhaps culpably, certain individuals have 'in their heads'. Despite the element of risk here (one student, for example, visited the counselling service saying Durkheim had been the final straw) this lecturer has a clear rationale for her practice. The function of university education, in her view, is to help students make sense of their lives. Course evaluations suggest that on the whole her students value her courses, though a handful note that there tends to be something of an emphasis on the downside of life. The Dean of the Faculty has been heard to remark acidly on the difference between education and therapy.

Lecturer C is continually absorbed by the problem of how maximally to engage his students in the business of learning. He has an acute sense of which students speak too little in seminars and which too much, and of strategies for encouraging one group and restraining the other. For example, his seminars regularly include opportunities for discussion in pairs and fours, on the grounds that a student who has spoken in a small group will find it easier to speak in a large one. He deliberately blurs the boundary between the personal and professional, wanting students to see that his subject, History, is no mere dry, academic discipline but can inform and enhance the lives of those who study it. By offering occasional autobiographical sketches and vignettes he gives students a sense of 'where he is coming from': they are surprised to discover that he too was once a rather unpromising undergraduate, looking for the quickest way to dispatch an essay on Charlemagne. He can reliably be found in a particular pub on Friday lunchtimes, equally happy to discuss Louis XIV, the legalization of drugs or the fortunes of the University rugby team. He has scathing contempt for colleagues who only see students between set 'office' hours. ('That word "office"', he likes to remark, 'says it all'.) They in return accept that he is a good teacher who *likes* his students; some degree of unease, however, seems to accompany this acknowledgement.

It is not difficult to find acknowledgement in the research literature of the importance of relationships to learning in higher education, though the word 'relationship' is not always used. Gibbs (1992) for example distinguishes between what he calls 'deep' and 'superficial' learning and writes of the importance of the 'motivational context' of learning: this is 'established by the emotional climate of the learning' (p 10). This climate is fostered by appropriate interaction with others: 'It is often easier to negotiate meaning and to manipulate ideas with others than alone. The importance of discussion for learning is not a new idea, though there is precious little discussion in much of higher education'. (p 11)

What does Dearing make of the place of the relationship between university teachers and their students? The following passage can be taken as representative:

> 8.6 At a seminar with prominent researchers specialising in learning in higher education, we sought to identify what is distinctive about learning at the higher level. We heard that it can be defined as the development of understanding and the ability to apply knowledge in a range of situations. This requires information and the opportunity to engage in 'learning conversations' with staff and other students in order to understand and be able to use new concepts in a particular field. A successful student will be able to engage in an effective discussion or debate with others in that field, relying on a common understanding of terms, assumptions, questions, modes of argument, and the body of evidence. Learning also involves acquiring skills, such as analysis and communication, but these in isolation do not constitute learning.

This paragraph repays careful reading. The nearest that Dearing comes to acknowledging the importance of the relationship between lecturers and their students is in mention of the opportunity to engage in learning conversations. These are placed in inverted commas, presumably to dignify them with semi-technical status and distinguish them from anything as unscientific or uneducational as a normal conversation, taking place in a normal relationship. And when there is talk of the place of discussion or debate, naturally that is *effective* discussion and debate. No doubt it will be economical and to the point – the very conditions of discussion that are inimical to the formation of deep and significant human relationships. We should note that Dearing distances itself from the substance of this paragraph. The second sentence is prefixed by 'we heard': it is left unclear whether this is to be understood as preceding and qualifying the rest of the paragraph, or whether the indicative mood is resumed with the third (or fourth, or fifth) sentence. Thus the Report manages to avoid the question of whether such things as 'communication skills', in the last sentence, are the proper business of the university. This evasiveness takes not one form but several. First there is the ambiguity: is it Dearing or the prominent researchers who are sceptical about such skills? Secondly, it is said that acquiring skills in isolation does not constitute learning. Since obviously if you are acquiring skills you *are* learning something, is it really the Higher Learning – the work of the universities – that acquiring these skills does not constitute? Thirdly, if it is the *isolation* of skills that is the problem, then skills isolated from what? From each other? From the subject-content of which universities are traditionally the guardians and purveyors? Or from considerations of what such skills are used for? Joseph Goebbels, after all, possessed highly effective communication skills. Skills can be used in pursuit of humane ends and in the course of respect for other persons, or barbaric ends where other people are treated as things. That is why human relationships matter, why Dearing's evasiveness is not of merely grammatical interest, and why the subject of the next section is what it is.

ETHICS

'Effectiveness' and words related to it, such as 'efficiency', become central in a culture where the dominant activity is the devising of means to ends, where consideration of values, of the ends to which means lead, no longer takes place to any significant extent (for more about means and ends, see Chapter 3). They are, as was said above, the defining terms of instrumental or technicist rationality. If we cannot make sense of teaching relationships in terms of *effectiveness*, then, if talk of relationships and of effectiveness is actually at odds, then perhaps ethics is a way of thinking that will prove helpful. This is not to suggest something like an 'ethical audit', but to suggest a change of language. Ethics, after all, is centrally concerned with human relationships, and promises an adjudication of all partial solutions such as the forms of technicism promise, and it is ethical language that seems necessary if we are to do justice to what were called earlier the 'internal goods' of education. That is to say that not just any way of teaching people – of 'delivering education' – will do as long as it produces results. Excessive pressure or giving students a sight of the examination paper the day before are ruled out because education is typically characterized by a degree of respect for persons and by honesty. These are the internal goods that distinguish it from indoctrination or academic force-feeding.

Yet what, amid all the interest in ethics *in* higher education (business ethics, bioethics, environmental ethics... ethics has certainly escaped from the confines of Philosophy departments), has become of the ethics *of* higher education? Such explicit attention to ethical matters as one finds in recent debate in the UK on the future of higher education tends to be couched in terms of equality or equality of opportunity and social justice. Of the 93 recommendations of the Dearing Report, for example, only two use a readily recognizable language of ethics. Recommendation 49 is worth quoting in its entirety:

> We recommend that all institutions should, as part of their human resources policy, maintain equal opportunities policies, and, over the medium term, should identify and remove barriers which inhibit recruitment and progression for particular groups and monitor and publish their progress towards greater equality of opportunity for all groups.

Here it is immediately noticeable that the distinctively ethical force of offering equal opportunities is blunted by expressing these as policies (rather than, say, as principles), as if they might be found in the same section of the university's handbook as the smoking policy and the policy of using each envelope three times, and furthermore as policies which are part of a further policy – a human resources policy – rather than a distinctively and avowedly ethical stance. In similar fashion the commitment to identifying and removing barriers 'which inhibit recruitment and progression' for disadvantaged groups loses some of its ethical edge through the suggestion that at the heart of the business is the desire to 'monitor and publish' – to survey, accumulate data and advertise an image – as opposed to rectifying injustices because they are *unjust*.

In any case, the foregrounding of equality and justice (Recommendation 60 concerns handling complaints from students in such a way as to reflect the principles of natural justice) highlights one particular dimension of ethics: that which is rights-based and quasi-contractual. Compare David Robertson (1997: 79) in a chapter entitled 'Social justice in a learning market': 'Public institutions which are not defined in terms of social justice [*defined* thus, we note, and not simply taking social justice as one more aim they pursue], accessible, accountable, fair to internal and external clients, responsive to public need, are not institutions which will easily attract support over the long term'. A university system which is ethically responsive is on this picture one which does right by its clients. Its contracts, both literal and metaphorical, are well-drafted and consistently honoured, no doubt reducing the danger of its clients making complaints. The bargain holds between the university's supply of services (degrees, consultancy etc) and the student's supply of income, whether directly or by proxy.

Such a picture of the ethically well-founded university should come as no surprise after the years in which the 'customers' of education, as of the other public services, have been vigorously reminded of their rights and encouraged to demand them, both by the publication of a series of 'charters' (student's and parent's in the field of education) and by the repeated reminders that the 'producer culture' of those who work in the public services (lecturers, teachers, doctors) constitutes an unhealthy monopoly. And it is unsurprising in the light of the kind of notion of ethics and ethical matters that currently prevails. All those burgeoning ethics which we mentioned near the start of this section (business ethics, etc; we recently came across a course on the ethics of speech and language therapy) tend to lend themselves principally to expression in terms of contracts and rights: putative rights of animals and embryos, patients and future generations.

This version of ethics and how it should inform the work of the university is all very well. It is necessary, we might say, but far from sufficient. To glimpse its limitations, consider what idea of ethics it conveys to those who pass through the university: what kind of moral or ethical education it constitutes. (We tend to think of moral education as proper to schools rather than as taking place in higher education, but we always absorb some kind of moral lesson from workplace and community. Misleadingly, this process now tends to be described as 'socialization'.) It is likely to convey a strong sense of the importance of adhering to an appropriate code, or meeting your obligations in respect of 'your side of the bargain'. As a student you work reasonably diligently, are punctual with your assignments; you participate actively in seminars, careful not to offend the sensibilities of minority groups and aware that there are others who for various historical and cultural reasons do not find it so easy to assert their point of view.

The lecturers, in return, fulfil their obligations. Their course outlines are clear, their objectives well-formulated; their teaching methods are varied and appropriate, as are their assessment strategies. Assignments are returned, and due feedback given, in reasonable time. Lecturers too have learned the protocol of equal opportunities. Unlike earlier generations of dons they do not distinguish 'girls' from 'men' in their audience, nor assume that their students have Christian names, nor caution single parents against taking a course that makes heavy demands. As far as the ethics of higher education is concerned, both parties here are in good standing. Now if this is the ethical character of the university of the future the first thing to note is that in comparison with some of the insensitivities and injustices of the past it has quite a lot to be said for it. But this is not what the students we heard at the beginning of this chapter were looking for, nor is it what the lecturers we sketched were moved by as an ideal.

The practice of these lecturers has a richness and complexity entirely missing from the 'contractual' view of staff–student relations. In all three cases there is (in different measures) a kind of alertness, a deep *attentiveness* to students as individuals, a determination to do *justice* to the tricky business of teaching and learning, and a resolve to be true to the nature of the material taught, the subject or discipline. In being aware of the difficulty of striking the right balance among these elements there is a refusal to settle for any complacent solution to the question of what exactly university education is for. Above all, perhaps, those who teach in the university in this way maintain a kind of continual awareness of the relationship between teacher and taught. That relationship is by no means unproblematic, as each sketch above indicates towards its end. Yet here there are no gains to be made unless a degree of risk is taken. Good teaching at all levels requires courage, amongst other virtues. This is another dimension of its ethical richness.

Perhaps it seems odd to talk of university teaching in these terms: to insist, as we are doing, that it is importantly and irreducibly ethical in its nature. If this does seem odd perhaps that is partly because our sense of what 'ethics' or 'morality' includes has shrunk so dramatically in recent times. We tend now to think of moral issues arising in circumscribed ways on particular occasions: about abortion, euthanasia or genetic engineering, for example, and when people are confronted with specific dilemmas. And, as writers like MacIntyre (1980) and Bernard Williams (1985) have shown us, our idea of 'morality' has narrowed. The more we see it as essentially a matter of obligations, rights and principles the less it helps us to make sense of the broad ethical demands which the modern world makes. A more adequate and serviceable version of ethics would focus less closely on the institutions (obligations etc) of morality. It would make room for consideration of the virtues, and of what constitutes a personally fulfilling life, including concern for self alongside concern for others.

To recall the significance of the *ethical* dimension of higher education, then, is not to appeal to the authority of a settled and authoritative system of thought in order to repair an educational institution whose own authority and purpose are increasingly in question. The scope and role of 'ethics' is at least as contentious as those of the university itself. More than that, it may be that their fortunes are linked: that our sense of the nature and importance of higher education has diminished in the same way and for much the same reasons that we are less and less inclined to be impressed by the force of distinctly ethical questions. If this is so, why persist in seeing the issue in ethical terms?

One way of answering that question is to note that alternative and currently favoured approaches have a way of reinstating the very problem that seemed in need of a solution. Imagine, for example, that there was widespread agreement that the new conditions of higher education are depriving students of learning experiences once available to them. Unable to form any real personal relationship with lecturers and tutors whose names they may barely know (and are seldom known by), they are correspondingly less able to experience and internalize the norms, values and methods of the subject or discipline of study. (These are the terms in which the matter is likely to be expressed.) Or they find it difficult to make any connections between their own individual lives and modules 'packaged' in such a way as to be offered across faculties, to franchised further education colleges, to distance learners in other countries. What more natural solution, then, than to offer a further module, in 'Personal Learning', say, or one addressing the theory of the subject or discipline in question? Here the solution, clearly, institutionalizes the very fragmentation that was the concern.

To put the matter in this way is to remind ourselves of a familiar point in current critique of the way that higher education is conceived. That point, alluded to earlier, is that a particular version of rationality – rationality as technicist and instrumental – has taken over and come to dominate our notions of reason, of the life of the mind, and so too our notions of the university. Barnett, for example, who is perhaps the best-known exponent of this view, writes:

> I contend that we are currently witnessing a shift in our sense of what it is to know the world of a fundamental kind. In essence, the shift is a move away from contemplative versions of knowledge to pragmatic and operational versions of knowledge... a move in our ways of knowing the world from knowing that to knowing how...What counts as knowledge is what is seen to have instrumental effects of appropriate kinds in the world, preferably effects which are likely to

promote a society of continuing change and which are likely to aid economic competitiveness. (1997: 39)

Barnett writes too of the 'missing vocabulary' (1997) of higher education: words such as 'critique' and 'wisdom' fall out of the discourse, and associated practices vanish with them. One way of understanding this chapter is as arguing that the language of ethics has become a significant, perhaps the most significant, 'missing vocabulary'. Only the thinnest ethical talk, as noted above, remains. If it has become difficult to use the language of ethics to defend things that are worth defending, is there any other language we can use?

DEMOCRACY

The idea of democracy by contrast has from the earliest times (for example, from Pericles's funeral oration in Book II of Thucydides's *History of the Peloponnesian War*) been connected with the idea of learning. A democratic society has been thought of as one where since all could speak all could be learnt from, and where the toleration of all kinds of opinion and styles of life (the Athenians live free 'from any jealousy, touching each other's daily course of life; not offended at any man, for pleasing himself', in Hobbes's translation of Thucydides, II.37) also means there is a rich diversity of resources and examples to learn from.

The insight that human relationships and the higher forms of learning are bound up together is one of the central ideas of the American philosopher John Dewey. He writes (Dewey, 1937) that democracy is more than just a way of conducting government and making laws. It is the best way that has yet been found for the development of the human personality, the 'full development of human beings as individuals'. Dewey articulates the connection between democracy and 'freed intelligence', the role of our social and political lives in cultivating the qualities of mind that we bring to choice and debate. We are not to be thought of as bringing our preformed selves and their choices into the public realm, as if freedom of action there was all we needed to be autonomous agents in a mature democracy. Rather is it the case that the kind of public realm we have – the society which Margaret Thatcher famously declared not to exist – shapes ourselves and our choices. Democracy does more for us than just enable us to pursue our individual choices and ends more successfully since we enjoy the co-operation of our fellows. A democratic society is the forum that stands to enrich our sense of what those ends and choices might themselves be.

Thus democracy is founded on faith in the power of 'pooled and co-operative experience'. Through democratic, open relationships, as opposed to autocratic and authoritarian ones, however benign, we learn from and with one another. We can know things in this way, in combination with one another, that we cannot know alone. Unless democratic habits of thought and action are part of 'the fiber of a people', Dewey writes, political democracy is insecure. Political democracy must be supported by democratic approaches to all social relationships. 'The relations that exist in educational institutions are second only in importance in this respect to those which exist in industry and business…'.

Above all, Dewey insists that education is not a one-way process, in which the educator brings techniques, however good (effective) to bear on the learner for his or her edification. 'Education consists primarily in transmission through communication. Communication is a process of sharing experience till it becomes a common possession. *It modifies the disposition of both the parties who partake in it'* (our emphasis). The relation between teacher and taught is a dialogical one. The significance of forms of human association, Dewey continues, lies in the contribution they make to the quality of experience. We look to the association between older and younger persons to provide a quality of experience which is itself educative, as well as employing more direct forms of teaching. As it appears all the time that there is more and more subject-matter in need of direct transmission, more curriculum for the teacher to 'deliver', this insight, that quality of experience is what is crucial, becomes more at risk of being lost: 'This danger was never greater than at the present time, on account of the rapid growth in the last few centuries of knowledge and technical modes of skill'.

Now Dewey has become anathematized, on both sides of the Atlantic, as 'the source of our schools' problems rather than the source of their solutions' (Schrag, 1995: 2). He is held responsible for woolly-headed ideas to the effect that children will learn best by 'discovery'; those whose views on education emphasize the importance of *content* – of the subject-matter to be learned – object to what they see as the excessive foregrounding of *process*, that is the view that we should attend to relationships in education as much as we have suggested we should in higher education. Whatever influence Dewey may or may not have had on schooling, however, his insights about the connections between democracy and learning seem important ones. What vision of the connections between democracy and university education do we find in Dearing?

Dearing has boldly accepted that drawing the connections between democracy and higher education is one of its tasks. In particular there is a strong emphasis on providing equal opportunities and on combating social exclusion, and Dearing does not duck discussion of the difficult issue of the 'common culture' – of what it is and to what extent it is the job of the universities to supply it. Nevertheless one of the most remarkable features of what Dearing has to say on democracy is its strongly individualistic bias. For example, under the heading *Higher education today* we read that part of the task of higher education is 'to accept a duty of care for the well-being of our democratic civilisation, based on respect for the individual and respect by the individual for the conventions and laws which provide the basis of a civilised society'. In itself this is unobjectionable, but perhaps it is ironic in view of what we have said are the essential connections between democracy and the quality of relationships. The failure to make room for truly educative *relationships* emerges even more strongly in Professor Stewart Sutherland's invited contribution (5.47). It is another of those extracts which deserves to be read with a critical attention that can easily be disarmed by the general impression of good sense that prevails throughout it:

> Higher education's central contribution to civic virtue is first and foremost in the spread of sense and practical wisdom in our society. Sense includes the capacity to distinguish truth from falsehood, knowledge from opinion, and good argument from bad. All of these fall within the tradition which emphasises the cultivation of the powers of the mind as central to all levels of education. Practical wisdom is the capacity to apply these to the needs of others as well as oneself in the time and place in which one lives.

It would be easy not to notice what is excluded. We apply sense, the powers of the mind and so on to the needs of others as well as to ourselves: what we do not do, apparently, is cultivate and apply these things *together*, in greater strength and wisdom than if we were to do so, as Professor Sutherland seems to envisage, separately. He continues:

> Democracy presupposes all of these abilities which is why the growth of democracy and the extension of education have always gone hand in hand. This is part and parcel of the responsibility which all citizens share in maintaining common purpose and the degree of common culture which is the foundation of democratic society.

In our time, however, there is an additional and distinctive role for our higher education institutions. A central challenge to democracy is the extension of specialised knowledge and its application to the way in which we live. Increasingly citizens are required to take, or at least to sanction very complex decisions about for example, nuclear power, about the most appropriate monetary system for our society, about complex moral issues surrounding gene therapy or reproductive biology, and so on. To do this with any confidence requires for each of us, to a varying degree, a combination of understanding and trust in the understanding of others. Higher education institutions have a dual responsibility in maintaining and strengthening these pillars of democracy.

After a paragraph from which Dewey might not dissent about the intrinsic connection between education and democracy, and the importance of common purpose and common culture, we return to the highly individualistic picture again. In our world of increasingly specialized knowledge we require two things: our own understanding and, where that fails, 'trust in the understanding of others'. The idea that higher education institutions have a responsibility also to foster educative relationships and foremost among them dialogue, the third way between the understanding of the isolated individual and his or her reliance on others, is, in the light of a reading of Dewey, noticeable by its absence.

We see here just one example, perhaps, of how the individualistic bias of late twentieth-century society has had the most far-reaching effects, influencing higher education along with all other parts of public life. (The fundamental individualism of current conceptions of higher education are explored further in Chapter 3.) Neo-Darwinian assumptions about competition and the 'survival of the fittest', coupled with the rejection of Keynesianism and the rise of neo-liberal theories of the economy, have led to the denigration of ideals of co-operation and community, the denial that there is any such thing as 'society'. All this is too familiar to be worth rehearsing here. But, it may be objected, isn't the world for which higher education is preparing its students a highly individualistic and competitive one, for which they need to learn to behave in individualistic and competitive ways? Chapter 3 argues that this line of thought provides no easy rebuttal of the case for the importance of relationships in higher education.

6

The Regional and Community
Role of Universities

Recurrently in this book we have stressed the importance for higher education of the relationships between people. Although recent reports include fairly frequent references to teamwork, to collaboration, and more generally to community, for the most part this is a matter that arises somewhat obliquely. There is a danger that what is really at issue is covered over, that a kind of tokenism takes the place of the more penetrating analysis that these complex matters call for if they are to mean much. In this chapter our intention is to extend this theme by considering ways in which personal relationships figure in the community role of the university. In the light of the positions adopted and the recommendations made in policy documents, we consider how far the conclusions we draw regarding the community role are significant also for questions of regional development focused more on the development of business and industry.

For university students over the past 50 years the typical experience of going to university has involved just that: going away to an institution to live and study for a period of three or four years. In many ways the experience of going away from home and of living with other students – especially in halls of residence but also in the shared houses and digs which students otherwise occupy – has been seen as a crucial part of higher education. It is clear that that pattern has changed in recent years with more students attending their local university and not moving away from the family home. Of the various factors that have contributed to this there are three that stand out. First, there is the change in the age profile of students. Between 1987 and 1992 applications from students over 21 increased by 215 per cent compared to a rate of increase of 66 per cent for those under 21 (Blackstone, 1997a: 22). More than half the students currently attending courses in higher education are mature. Many have family circumstances or other commitments that make moving away from the locality undesirable or impossible. Second, there are the changes in the funding and support for students in higher education, causing some students to try to cut costs by continuing to live at home and by studying at their local institution. Given the support that this policy has received in Parliament and the muted opposition from the National Union of Students itself, this is likely to be policy for the foreseeable future. Third, there is the growth of part-time courses, with over a third of all students now falling into this category. Apart from regular modes of part-time study it seems likely that the future will bring more wide-scale changes with more irregularity in patterns of attendance. Baroness Blackstone suggests that 'Lifelong learning puts a premium on universities being accessible throughout the year to allow people to study when they are not working. The university of the 21st century will probably be open for students for 50 weeks a year' (1997a). As students move in and out of university study in the course of their careers, and in view of the costs incurred, it is likely that more study will be part time. Alongside these points it should be acknowledged that technological change is having effects, albeit of an ambiguous kind. On the one hand, local universities can set themselves up as learning centres providing the technical means for the accessing of learning online. On the other, and more significantly, the courses themselves – or some of their study material, which is not the same thing – are increasingly likely to be distributed on a global scale and available to anyone with access to the Internet. These factors all relate in some degree to a significant if partial change in the social class profile of university students. The extension of opportunity to more people may have meant that higher education has lost some of its mystique: for many it may now be regarded as a route to qualifications and a job and as something less than the major formative experience that it once was. Whatever dilution of the experience this may represent, however, this is not to deny the desirability of the extension of opportunity to more people. One consequence of these changes, then, has been a new emphasis on the local and regional role of the university. Recognizing that an increasing number of students are likely to be recruited locally, many universities are changing their marketing accordingly, though perhaps not without anxiety about the consequences of this for their profile on the national and international stage. It is the implications of this local role that will be explored in the present chapter.

As we have indicated, this has coincided with a new emphasis on the role of universities in relation to business development in the region. To a great extent these changes have been driven by concerns over economic competitiveness. The vision of the future development of a knowledge-based economy and investment in human capital set out in the Green Paper on Lifelong Learning takes the development of higher and further education to be crucial to the achievement of both economic prosperity and social cohesion. The Dearing Report's calls for higher education to be responsive to the needs of local industry and commerce (Recommendation 37) have been met by assertions of commitment on the part of the Government to the embedding of 'a culture in which higher education and business see themselves as partners in enhancing human capital' (The Learning Age: http://www.lifelonglearning.co.uk). The desire to break down old divides extends to the removal of barriers between the academy and business. The Government has asserted the need for better use of existing links in consultancy, research, and knowledge transfer; for more technology 'incubator units' within or close to the institution, within which start-up companies can be fostered for a limited period until they are able to stand alone (Recommendation 39); for work experience for all students. All this requires closer co-operation.

Although a distinction is maintained between the aim of economic competitiveness and that of individual development, this is a further divide that the idea of lifelong learning seeks to erode. It is not just that lifelong learning is desirable if the country is to have a suitably skilled and adaptable workforce: rather a new relation to work is implied. In a way, and in presentational terms, this necessitates a kind of conjuring trick: in the early 1980s the local Job Centre became a point of social focus, the often painful emblem of the aspiration to work and the lack of real jobs; in the late 1990s the stigma of the Job Centre needs to be superseded by the High Street Learning Shop with its symbolism of open availability, opportunity, and empowerment, and its customer-oriented ambience. Of course, the significance of this change is all the more critical precisely in circumstances of social disadvantage, and the various methods that have been used to extend access and to re-present institutions as 'community universities', especially in such areas, have been important moves towards the kind of sea change that the culture of social inclusion requires.

The desire to overcome the disjunction of economic competitiveness and personal fulfilment here is matched by the attempt to show the congruence of the benefits of education for the individual and for society at large. The Green Paper on Lifelong Learning makes clear the Government's commitment to a partnership in the development of post-compulsory education involving both the individual and the wider community:

> 1.1 The Fryer report called for a transformation of culture to achieve the Learning Age. The Government endorses that call and this consultation paper is the beginning of that process. Transforming our learning culture will depend on a partnership between individual responsibility and the wider community. As individuals and enterprises increasingly take charge of their own learning and of meeting their need for skills, they will require support to enable them to achieve their goals, including better access.

> 1.2 In future, learners need not be tied to particular locations. They will be able to study at home, at work, or in a local library or shopping centre, as well as in colleges and universities. People will be able to study at a distance using broadcast media and on-line access. Our aim should be to help people to learn wherever they choose and support them in assessing how they are doing and where they want to go next.

> 1.3 Demand is potentially vast. When asked, companies and individuals say they want to improve their skills. And many do. People learn for a variety of reasons; it could be to change career, to increase earning power, to update skills, or simply for the joy of learning itself. Last year about eight million adults studied in colleges, universities, on training courses delivered by Training and Enterprise Councils (TECs) or at evening classes. This is a good start, but we must do better. Many more people could be involved in learning but are not because they face barriers. We are seeking views on how these can be overcome.

The commitment to promote wider access is in part a new drive for social cohesion. On the one hand, it is recognized that in the knowledge economy of the future those without education are likely to be progressively excluded. On the other, the divisive nature of progression to higher education, linked as this so clearly is to social class, is increasingly acknowledged. Thus, the regional and community role of the university has an important bearing not only on matters of economic regeneration and growth but also on matters of social identity.

In his recent review of New Labour's agenda and performance in relation to lifelong learning, Josh Hillman has drawn attention to the fact that the centrality of lifelong learning to the competitiveness of the workforce and to economic regeneration has been articulated at the highest levels. (Indeed on 29 May 1998 the *Times Higher Education Supplement* ran a front-page item by Alan Thomson with the title 'Lifelong learning ace in Treasury poker game'. It begins: 'Universities will be asked to throw their weight behind the government's lifelong learning agenda as part of the battle to secure more funding from this summer's comprehensive spending review'.) The principle of lifelong learning is to be seen as one of three strands, alongside labour market flexibility and welfare reform, in the 'strategic "third way" for twenty-first century centre-left politics, between the social regulation and inclusivity of continental European social-democratic models and the dynamism and flexible markets of North America' (Hillman, 1998: 65). Hillman sees lifelong learning policy as crucial to New Labour's political philosophy in terms of its significance for social justice. It is a means of addressing the social exclusion of those lacking marketable skills: equipping people with such skills will provide access to the labour market and income mobility, factors that will be critical for their life-chances. Although broadly supportive of current change, Hillman suggests, perhaps with some regret, that radicalism is confined to the flagship policies of the University for Industry and Individual Learning Accounts – both of which are praised as appropriate responses to the fact that 'we cannot expect to raise educational levels simply by increasing throughput via existing channels' (Hillman, 1998: 68). Nevertheless he is optimistic about lifelong learning's potential, not least in the ways that it can give the learner greater control:

> If individuals are given greater responsibility for their learning, the other side of the coin is that they should have greater control over the location, context and processes of their learning. The components of this are already familiar or exist in embryo. A national credit framework, linking FE and HE, would supplant the fixed hierarchies of existing awards and give students greater flexibility over when, what and where they study. Unfortunately the 'Learning Age' works with the grain of many existing credit framework developments, which have tended to split FE from HE. What is needed is a credit framework which links learning at all levels and allows for flexible progression (Robertson, 1994). At the same time, student-centred learning should replace subject-based teaching, the boundaries of which have already been transformed. (Hillman, 1998: 68)

Hillman provides an upbeat assessment of the Government's performance to date and demonstrates his own commitment to the values that lifelong learning embodies. This affirmation of faith tends, however, to be somewhat limited in the justification it provides: lifelong learning is the way to economic competitiveness and to combating social exclusion. What is lacking is any real exploration of what social inclusion might consist in. And there is an uncritical acceptance of received ideas – of the new 'progressivism' in effect, as we saw in Chapter 2 – that means that the article leaves us with a somewhat hackneyed conception of lifelong learning which avoids the most important questions.

Hillman does make some valuable remarks about the regional role of educational institutions in the light of the creation of the Regional Development Agency (RDA) and the prospect of emerging regional government. He anticipates that the RDAs will play an important role in the co-ordination of activity and offer a forum for strategic foresight of tertiary education. He goes on:

> Regional development will be important not only to tertiary education and skills strategies but also to HE. HE institutions differ radically in their approach to their regions: the research elite consider themselves international players, not regional actors; others are defined extensively through their local and regional impact, particularly through the partnerships with employers and providers they construct at these levels. With the development of greater strategic purpose at the regional level, the likelihood is that the role of HE as a critical economic and social engine will strengthen, at the same time as different market differentiation emerges between institutions on the basis of the different audiences and client bases they address. (Hillman, 1998: 71)

In line with our own earlier remarks, Hillman draws attention to the ambivalence that some universities are currently experiencing: pressures to serve the local community and to work towards regional growth increase while more familiar roles are challenged on other fronts. We need to explore ways in which these new demands are reconciled with the kind of higher education that this book is seeking to defend. What questions and problems are raised by this understanding of lifelong learning and by the recommendations that are shaping government policy? With regard to economic regeneration there are questions concerning the relation between research and industry, questions of collaboration and competition, of trust and confidence; there are questions of location and accessibility; and there are questions concerning the usefulness or otherwise of higher education. With regard to service to individuals in the community, there are questions of access and of modes of attendance, and there is the broader matter of the social focus that the university can acquire. Embedded in these matters are questions concerning how the individual and the community are best able to flourish. It is to the nature of that connection and of the kinds of relationship that need to be involved that we now turn.

COMMUNITY AND FRIENDSHIP

During the 1990s all the major political parties have made their attempts to appropriate the idea of community. With the reaction to the effects of the free market capitalism initiated by the governments of Ronald Reagan and Margaret Thatcher and with the political tiredness that ensued, community seemed like an idea whose time had come. Both Bill Clinton and Tony Blair drew on the ideas of Amitai Etzioni, and a 'fluffy rhetoric' of community become commonplace (see Pahl and Spencer, 1997). It is clear that if the idea is to be of value it requires a finer and less sentimental characterization than these ways of speaking permit. Moreover, it needs to be understood in the light of the reality of social change, a reality that disrupts some of the settled pictures of harmony that the notion is apt to evoke.

As Pahl and Spencer point out, traditional forms of marriage, family and community have altered and it is necessary to build on what *is*, rather than on what ought to be. There is an increasing bridging out and away from the weak ties of traditional communities and this hastens social change. As family and kinship ties weaken and fragment, the importance of other sorts of personal relationship increases. It is to friends that many people turn in times of crisis or on occasions for celebration, for example, and in relation to whom they increasingly come to identify themselves. (Witness the current popularity of the television series *Friends*.) Although this trend is viewed with suspicion by some, as hastening the breakdown of stable family relationships, there are ways in which the change reflects values that go to the heart of human nature and community. There is often a more or less automatic reaction to such change, prompted by insecurity perhaps, which is blind to the more laudable aspects of the impulses behind it. Thus the decline – so it is commonly perceived – in marriage itself may indicate ways in which people have become more demanding in relationships: they see them as all the more central to their personal fulfilment and seek a confluence that was less commonly expected in the past. While family ties may weaken and become somewhat 'forced', it is to be recognized that there can be an authenticity to friendship and that this does not normally begin with the obligations of family connection. True friendship can develop free of the guilt and ambivalence characteristic of family life. Of course, friendships of a limited kind may have a functional character, where we mix with people for particular limited pursuits (eg to play squash), but these are marginal. Pahl and Spencer refer to the three characteristics in

Aristotle's account: friends enjoy each other's company; they do useful things for each other; and they help each other to lead better lives. Within these criteria there is the basis of a politics of friendship. True friends help us to form and affirm our identities and provide essential threads that bind our lives together.

Pahl and Spencer suggest that a concept other than community is needed to refer to the kinds of relationship depicted here which are so important to people in the course of their lives and they suggest that this is provided by the notion of *social convoy*: 'As we move through life there is a changing cluster of significant others who provide affective, relational and normative support as we move through the life course... [This might serve as] a term for the real, as opposed to the imagined, sets of relationship that people carry with them through their lives' (1997: 104). Social convoys provide continuities of personal relationship of the kind that are essential to us. Crucial to Aristotle's account of friendship is the idea that our friends help us to lead better lives through sharing with us the commitment to certain goods. Social convoys, themselves constituted by friendships, play such a role. As Pahl and Spencer aim to show, these types of relationship are central and important in the contemporary world, and they have the potential, if properly recognized, to lead to a more moral and a more cohesive society:

> It is our contention that there is now substantial evidence that we are living in a society that is increasingly based on friend-like relationships of choice. People are becoming more sophisticated in recognising the subtleties of forms of social exchange and reciprocity. Instead of the taken-for-granted nature of ascribed roles, people are questioning the meaning of all types of traditional or ascribed relationships. Partners, siblings and adult children can all be seen as friends in the strongest Aristotelian sense. This, if encouraged, can develop the stronger moral community which political leaders seek. However, this is in the small sets of actual relationships in which people live and work out their identities. It is paradoxical that despite increasing globalisation our crucial social supports are in the micro-social worlds of action sets, support networks and bridging relationships. (Pahl and Spencer, 1997: 105–6)

Pahl and Spencer raise important points here and their exploration of friendship is a refreshing contribution to discussions of community. There are limitations to their account, however, especially concerning the lack of clarity that is given to the concept of friendship and the kind of policy implications that affirmation of its value might support. The article provoked a thoughtful response from Michael Fielding who takes up some of these points.

Although Fielding sees much that is of value in the arguments of Pahl and Spencer, he takes issue with them on two main fronts. First, the article fails to provide

> a convincing philosophical account of human being and becoming on which any adequate articulation of friendship or community must rest…Thus, it is not clear what the relation is, if any, between friendship and community. Are they now one and the same thing, and if not, are we to write off community as irretrievably unhelpful, doubtfully and questionably attainable, or both? And what of the insistence that we concentrate on what is or what works, rather than what ought to be? (Fielding, 1998: 56–7)

His second objection is that the account lacks clarity at the very point at which it is most needed, and that is the relation between the personal, the social, and the political. It does not provide hints as to what a 'friendship-friendly' social policy might mean. And regarding the politics of friendship, it does not address the problematic of a politics of friendship in a postmodern world so unlike the relatively homogeneous civic republicanism of Athens, the political backdrop to these ideas. Furthermore, there is no sense of the way that 'the very spontaneity and freedom entailed in friendship might sit uncomfortably within the framework of politics' (Fielding, 1998: 57).

To meet these shortcomings, Fielding argues, we need 'an emancipatory account of community at the heart of which lies an individuality conditional upon the kind of vibrant mutuality that friendship typically offers' (1998: 57). Such an account of community needs to help us not only to understand its nature but also its relation to the political, social, and personal dimensions of human experience. We need to gain some idea of how we might create community of the sort that is conducive to an inclusive human fulfilment.

Such an account is available, Fielding contends, in the work of the Scottish philosopher, John Macmurray. In Macmurray's view the notion of an unencumbered self is incoherent because of the insistent fact of our mutuality – we need other people in order to be or even to become ourselves. Certain kinds of human relationship enable us to be more fully ourselves and pre-eminent amongst them is friendship. This Macmurray regards as basic and universal. Essentially other-regarding, friendship cannot be justified in instrumental terms – indeed it is *the*

example, many would say, that shows the limits to instrumental justifications of things that we value – but must have its purpose in the mutual
expression of fellowship. And what he says here is equally applicable to
his account of community. The talk of community prevalent today, in
contrast, can mask less benign tendencies. For example, some communities (including those that are current in contemporary society) are characterized by hierarchy and repression; nostalgic notions of community
evoked by images of cricket on village greens and warm beer are irre-
trievably paternalistic. We need to avoid both 'the watchful self-
absorption of atomistic individualism and the earnest self-abrogation of
its organic counterpart' (Fielding, 1998: 63). Macmurray's conception, in
contrast, is emancipatory in that it recognizes the equality and freedom
that must lie at the heart of friendship if the constraints of fear and the
anxiety for control are not to undo or irrevocably to compromise it. His
account enables us to distinguish between the changing forms of our
relationships and the underlying energy and integrity that provide their
emancipatory edge. Because friendship is, as Fielding puts it,

> so intimately bound up with the conditions under which we can most
> fully be ourselves, friendship is for Macmurray 'the supreme value in
> life and the source of all other values' (Macmurray, 1929, p 5). It is the
> one true measure of success. Despite the quite other values which our
> society proclaims, he urges us to understand that our success 'will
> have only one measure; it will be measured by the extent and depth of
> your friendship with men and women. That alone will benefit the
> world; within that, and within that alone, all other value for yourself
> or the world will grow' (*ibid.* p 8) (Fielding, 1998: 59).

Macmurray draws a fundamental distinction between 'functional' and
'personal' relationships between people. Functional relationships exist
where, for example, a customer buys something in a shop, or where, on a
larger scale, people co-operate in a range of ways to achieve common
purposes in society. These more or less contractual relationships are
desirable in many ways and modern society is inconceivable without
them. In personal relationships, in contrast, people respond to each
other as whole persons and the relation exists for its own sake. Friendship exemplifies this while on a larger scale it is expressed in community,
which consists 'not in the conjunction of common purposes but in the
sharing of a common life' (Fielding, 1998: 60). Of course, in friendship
and community there will be, as Aristotle recognized, the practicalities
of purpose and action – we will help each other to do useful things – but
this is not the point of the relationship, and this is crucial. Such purposes

and actions will change but here, unlike in the case of functional rela-tionships, this change will not dissolve the relation. To the extent that the point of social, political, and economic activity is that people flourish, these are subordinate to community because that is the condition in which people can be most fully themselves. Thus, economic activity that is at the expense of the personal life is self-frustrating: 'the economic is for the sake of the personal' (Macmurray, 1961: 188). And there can be no politics of a democratic kind without the common way of life and the kind of trust that community provides.

If the development of a democratic polity depends on community in this way, and if community is both the end and the means of human fulfil-ment, how, Fielding asks, are we to go about achieving it? First, it needs to be clear, it cannot be ordered into existence any more than friendship can be imposed. Failure to recognize this has been responsible for some of the immense efforts and gigantic failures of social policy. Second, and recalling the remarks above concerning equality and freedom, we can recognize that there is a major obstacle to the growth of community where people live and work in conditions of fear. Third, although the functional life cannot create the personal life, the two are inextricably linked. Writing in 1941, Macmurray claims: 'The functional life is for the personal life; the personal life is through the functional life... the shape of the one decides the outlines of the other' (Macmurray, 1941a: 822). And in a remark a week later, 'The state is for the community; the com-munity is through the state' (Macmurray, 1941b: 856). Fielding sums up the significance of this well: 'The common stock of wealth that we pro-duce through our economic and political co-operation is the stuff out of which we can care for each other's material needs and it is the distribu-tion and use of this resource that provides an indispensable basis on which to judge the sincerity and the authenticity of our communal aspi-rations.' Our community becomes real through our willing co-operation in providing for one another's needs.

If these arguments are sound, there are disturbing implications for cur-rent thinking in relation to lifelong learning. For while the rhetoric there is one of empowerment and social inclusion, the consequences of the individual and a contextual practice that it endorses are a reduction in the possibility of precisely those relationships on which friendship and community depend. It is our contention here and elsewhere in this book (see especially Chapters 5 and 9) that what is at stake is not simply a mat-ter of social cohesion, of the harmony of a supposed community, but education itself; and a real community, we are inclined to say, can only flourish where the nature and the point of education are rightly understood. The quality of the relationships involved is crucial to the quality of education, something current indicators of quality are manifestly incapable of registering. Empowering the individual through giving her greater control over her learning, maximizing the availability of learning opportunities to her, may deprive her even as these apparent benefits seem most dedicated to her needs. Friendship and community depend not on giving her greater choice but on something different and more elusive. In fact they may require her rather to renounce her desire for control, in a tacit coming to terms with the fact that she is not a free-floating individual or an unencumbered self. Lifelong learning as it is currently promoted encourages her to think that she is, and that this is how she should be.

THE DEMANDS OF COMMUNITY AND REGIONAL DEVELOPMENT

The account of community drawn from Macmurray can, we believe, help us to understand the university in its local and regional role, and we shall show shortly the practical implications of the argument. Before that, however, it is appropriate to draw attention to two problems, actual or potential. In the first place, there is the danger that the account will seem to be endorsing a conception of community which is overly optimistic, whatever its protestations of realism. There is a sense of organic harmony, encouraged especially by the connection with friendship, and although this is appropriate up to a point it is important to resist the sentimentalization to which this might be prone. (Still more, we might add, to resist the kind of *Brideshead* nostalgia that the idea of the university community might evoke.) We want to draw attention not to the happiness or easiness of the relationships between people in community – indeed at times they can be demanding and difficult (as friendships can) – but to the fact that they must be personal and meaningful and involve the sharing of a common life. In the second place, it is important to recognize the danger that such an account of community may seem to cover over the complexities of the modern world and partially to erase the differences that characterize contemporary pluralistic society. These complexities are amplified through changes in technology, changes that alter so profoundly our relationship to time and space. Pluralism presents vividly to us what has perhaps always been true: that our lives are made up of interweaving strands involving multiple changing communities, that they are characterized as much by relations of what we might call partial connectivity as by participation in organic wholes. What we want to ask nevertheless is how far universities are or might become contributors to community in the sense that has been elaborated and how this might connect with their regional role.

What do universities in fact do in this respect? We have throughout this book acknowledged the variety of higher education and it is worth remembering that the challenges presented here will figure differently for different institutions. Different problems are faced by the traditional university with ancient buildings and a history of town-and-gown divisiveness, by the campus university cut off from the local town, and by the new university with its muddle of buildings strewn through the town but its strong record of local recruitment. In some cases universities will have a robust or perhaps self-conscious sense of their internal community and of their connections with the world beyond the immediate region; in others the role as a local employer, as an arts and sports centre, and as a provider of part-time courses will emphasize their dynamic role within the local area. Some universities then seem to be better placed to play, and indeed more experienced in playing, the kind of community role that is in question.

In the drive to remove barriers to access, we are reassured repeatedly by policy documents and commentators alike that the learners of the future will not be tied to particular places or, for that matter, particular times of study. The buildings of the university and their location will become increasingly insignificant as new technology begins to streamline and extend provision. There are good reasons to welcome this extension of opportunity, but it is also appropriate to reflect on the social effects of removing these constraints and the different experience of learning they provide. Students attending classes see others in the flesh: they share coffee breaks, get tired together, laugh or commiserate in the library, wait for the bus, and occasionally party. What happens when they are together cannot be dictated solely by the demands of the course, if only for reasons of physical need. They rub shoulders in ways that inevitably take them beyond anything that could be set down in a course specification or set of learning outcomes, yet this informal contact can be a vital part of their learning. Furthermore, as a venue for arts events, occasional conferences, sporting activity, and short courses the university can draw people into this kind of social space, where the focus of the activity, the very thing that brings them together, blends imperceptibly into shared patterns and rhythms of ordinary life. New technology and other forms of communication permit rich personal relationships of different kinds as we show in Chapter 7, but the point here is the way people are brought together in this complex social manner which exceeds the bounds of its ostensible purpose.

The Government has stressed, as we noted above, the need to establish 'a culture in which higher education and business see themselves as partners in enhancing human capital'. Our view is that it is necessary to explore ways of reconciling the new demands on higher education regarding its community and regional role with those academic commitments that this book is seeking to uphold. We doubt, to reiterate the point made in Chapter 1, that conceiving of these problems in terms of 'enhancing human capital' is conducive to thinking well about these matters. Our terms here are different, and we avoid the atomistic picture of the social world that recurs in the policy documents. It might be thought that in our emphasis on community and friendship we stress such factors as the personal growth and well-being of students in such a way as to be at odds with the role of the university in contributing to regional business development To show that this is not the case let us consider in a little more detail the ways that collaboration between universities and businesses might work and might indeed be mutually beneficial.

Dearing rightly emphasizes the ways in such collaboration between universities and industry can contribute to economic regeneration and growth. Collaboration of this kind includes the provision of courses geared to the recruitment demands of local industry, the development of research, the stimulation of industrial and business innovation, and, if the university's doors are appropriately open, many other possible ventures and forms of contact. The university can help local business to be competitive, it will be claimed; in our view there are other ways in which its contribution to their success will be most significant. Hillman argues that collaboration will lead to significant improvements in the quality of learning as well as exploitation of economies of scale (Hillman, 1998: 68). We want to press the idea of economies of scale beyond this all too familiar sense – of immediately calculable returns – to suggest that there are real benefits to be gained from creating conditions that foster development on a *local scale*. We have in mind what John Cantwell has identified as the 'tacit capability' necessary for businesses and industry to flourish, especially in the age of a globalized knowledge economy when R&D is so central to success.[1]

As Cantwell explains, 'Innovation consists primarily of the accumulation of *tacit capability* – sometimes termed "technological accumulation". Tacit capability is *embodied in social organisations*, mainly in firms, and so tends to be tied to production *by a specific set of firms in a particular location'* (Cantwell 1995, 66, italics added). Cantwell posits a connection between a different conception of technological knowledge (as 'tacit capability'), its embodiment in institutional communities, and its geographically specific location. This tacit capability is nourished both by innovatory R&D and by training and education, both directly or indirectly relevant to the firm's activities. If, as Cantwell further writes, 'profit through innovation has become even more important' with globalization (Cantwell, 1995: 67), then it seems to follow that globalization need not be destructive of local identity if it is intelligently understood and managed. Indeed, when discussing the specificity of national systems for innovation in science and technology, Cantwell explicitly claims that 'Contrary to what is sometimes alleged, globalisation and national specialisation are complementary parts of a common process, and not conflicting trends'. (Cantwell, 1995: 70).

Small to medium enterprises cannot reasonably develop their own R&D in isolation nor easily develop their own training packages, and so they particularly need the involvement of higher education. For while there are inevitable returns to firms from their own R&D and training, returns that large corporations can easily capture, for small or specialized firms the returns can be too small if the firm has to foot the whole cost. 'Therein', writes Cantwell,

> lies the role for public policy. By supporting education and training, governments help lower the costs and facilitate the creation of tacit capability. That is, government can address what is at root an institutional failing rather than a malfunctioning of the markets... Public research is not replacing some 'missing' private endeavour but acting as a catalyst for the widening of private research. (Cantwell, 1995: 69)

That, at least, is how it should be – not, as it seems increasingly in Britain, a matter of the private sector 'contracting out' its own work to the universities: 'What *innovative* companies expect from local universities is not research with immediate commercial application in their own sector, but rather a wider base of knowledge creation and skills with which their own facilities can interact' (Cantwell 1995: 69, italics added). And what is 'in it' for the universities themselves? Once firms are drawing on the output of higher education to form and strengthen their tacit capability, then 'In practice, there is continual interaction between learning in production (innovation) and research and science, but on the whole there tend to be more links that run from technology in production to research and to science than the other way round… An illustration is the impact of computer technology on scientific enquiry.' (Cantwell, 1995: 68)

On this optimistic account, then, it may seem that the universities need not fear erosion of their academic functions if their relation with industry is the one that is best for industry itself; and they can in fact gain from the process in their own academic terms. Cantwell's emphasis on the fact that tacit capability is embodied in social organizations has an interesting bearing on the reflections of this chapter in that the kinds of contact that local connections make possible are different from those that are available at a distance. Think, for example, of the role of day conferences, workshops and other forms of continuing professional development. His emphasis on the way that tacit capability tends to be tied to production by a specific set of firms in a particular location underlines the importance of place – of community, if you like – in a way that is usually overridden by faith in the potential of new technology. The difficulty here is gaining a perspective on this issue that does justice to the globalizing effects and beneficial potential of new technology for overcoming the barriers of distance while at the same time remaining open-eyed about the very real significance that locatedness has for human beings.

We need to remember the kinds of contacts that people have when they live and work in the same locality and the quality of the relationships that can then be generated – how colleagues, for example, often become friends. This is partly the inadvertent outcome of the physical proximity and social contact that such situations permit. But a further factor figures here. Jean Renoir once remarked that a French farmer would have more to talk about with a farmer in China than with a city worker in Paris. Having a common purpose and having occasion to discuss it brings people into a kind of relation where the threads of common life can sometimes be drawn together.

The discussion in this chapter, as in Chapter 5, points to the importance of trust. In conditions of fear and anxiety, it was said, friendship and community are unlikely to flourish. There is no doubt that much business activity depends on a kind of trust, whatever popular images of hardheadedness might imply. And perhaps we should be less than wholly cynical about its appropriation of certain value terms. 'Confidence' may refer ostensibly to the state of the money markets and the stability of interest rates, but it can also imply something more, and marketing increasingly realizes this. 'Hospitality' as a means of promoting sales involves the kind of informal, varied, and necessary activity that, beyond any merely calculative intentions, provides the contacts out of which friendship can grow. Getting people together, putting people in touch (the phrase is significant), offers the primary conditions of community. Involving them in the varied activities that go with hospitality creates possibilities of relationship that stretch in unpredictable ways beyond the business at hand.

You cannot create community, but you can remove fear. You can create conditions where people come into contact with one another socially. And you can create conditions where what brings them together, in freedom from the anxious tentacles of control, is the shared pursuit of something perceived to be good, in service even of something higher. This, as we have tried to show in Chapter 2, is exactly what the study of academic subjects should be. (And subjects are public goods, quite unlike inert commodities in which individual stakeholders might invest.) Social policy can create conditions where the functional life and the personal life have the potential to develop in harmony: where the functional life is for the personal life; the personal life is through the functional life.

The Fryer Report argues that there must be a shift of focus from institutions and onto individuals. Dismantling institutions, we fear, diminishes the possibilities of that harmony and that community. For the university has a place in our communities that is in many respects still to be realized, and that place is not just a location but rather a *topos*[2], one that might occasion opportunities for growth more significantly than the virtual location of the University for Industry ever could. All the Utopian claims for the latter merely point to the fact that it is the university of no place (it is literally *utopos*): it cannot provide the public realm through which the community and the region can best be served.

Notes

1. For a fuller discussion of these ideas in relation to higher education see Blake, 1998.
2. A *topos* is a focus for activity that draws together patterns of regional connection. It is not to be understood in terms of a location on a grid but rather in terms of the part it plays and the meaning it has in people's lives. ('The university in our town has a place [*topos*] at the heart of our

community.') It is worth noting that the English language is apt to make this sense of place appear merely metaphorical.

7

The Management of Learning

The phrases 'the management of teaching' and 'the management of learning' are much in the air at the moment. They permeate the Dearing Report, for instance, and are loudly echoed in further education as earnests of innovatory zeal and political acceptability. The first phrase is the very kind of thing that rings alarm bells for those concerned for academic freedom. But 'the management of learning' has an Orwellian ring to it. For, like all things truly Orwellian, it can sound superficially benign. After all, learning is not a simple matter and learning is arguably more difficult than ever it has been, in a modern culture so profuse in knowledge, so rich in detailed argument, so astoundingly specialized, so complex in its interdisciplinary possibilities. Such complications call for management, some may say – only those determined to see the figure of the manager as overtly or covertly authoritarian can recoil at the thought of the management of learning or doubt it as a major benefit to students, and indeed a progressive and disinterested one. Indeed, a long tradition of books of advice on how to study provide, in effect, useful and well-tried nostrums for self-management in learning.

The attraction, to some, of the project of managing learning seems to be the prospect of it replacing teaching, in part or perhaps even wholly. Under conditions of mass participation in higher education, schemes for the management of learning can be addressed to large groups of students simultaneously. Thus management may seem to have the potential to be of benefit to more students than old-fashioned face-to-face tuition. And if such economic advantages loom – if the manager of learning can be effective and efficient in ways that no tutor or lecturer could possibly be – then one starts looking also to justifications of him or her in terms of pedagogy. Might not the manager of learning be potentially a less directive or manipulative figure, allowing greater liberty for self-directed and thus enriched learning? Besides, how are students to acquire the self-direction and initiative they will eventually need to piece together credibly their own career of training and retraining in the Learning Society if they are still, at their age, subject to the direction of teachers? Indeed, with burgeoning numbers of mature and adult students, is it even truly tolerable that such students bend to the tutelage of being 'taught'? A discreet and disinterested management of their learning might be more compatible with their adult autonomy. Do not students actually need facilitators rather than teachers? Perhaps academics need to become facilitators? Perhaps we need even to replace them by others who are facilitators and expressly not academics.

Educational radicalism in the 1970s was often characterized by paranoid distrust of teaching as an ideological imposition, as a covert power game between innocent student and coercive teacher. Ironically, it seems that distrust may yet find its fulfilment in the very kind of managerialism the radicals used to oppose. The management of learning seems to some to offer the same restraint on teaching, or even its demise, that the radicals used to long for. What are we to make of this? Were the radicals moving in the right direction for the wrong reasons? Or are the new managers of learning as wrong as the radicals, and as dangerous?

One problem which made radical arguments against teaching so overtly implausible in their day was the question of what would fill its place – to which the radical answer was so often 'Well nothing, really! Just give us the libraries (or not)'. What's different now, of course, is the explosion of information technology. What takes the place of the teacher might be interactive multimedia software, teaching packages delivered by audio and videotape, CD-ROM, videodisk, and of course the omnipresent Internet. Now, new technologies do indeed seem to put the very necessity of teaching in question. Management may seem more benign at last.

And should this worry us anyway? If higher education involves the pursuit of knowledge and the optimal dissemination of learning, then all means are grist to its mill, for it seeks not some ideal terminus but the continual opening of further doors to knowledge and understanding for an ever-widening constituency. It goes without saying that information technology (IT) will – already does – impinge fruitfully on higher education. But technologies applied indiscriminately can be counterproductive. What the technologist proposes is for the educator to dispose. And, currently, we seem to be in a state of deep and dangerous confusion about the appropriate role both for IT and for the management of learning, in higher and other tertiary education.

If the management of learning marginalizes the role of the teacher – or, in more benign versions, frees the teacher from routines for more worthwhile teaching activities – nonetheless it needs a philosophy of learning to justify its methods. This is what we need to assess, its proper role and that of its new ally, IT. Many are currently tempted to look to some kind of philosophy of Open Learning for this; not least because there are an increasing number of departments and institutions which already describe themselves as running Open Learning schemes. In particular, there are those who refer to the Open University as an Open Learning institution – misleadingly, we shall argue – and draw on its prestige to invoke credibility for their own Open Learning schemes (so called). 'More of the same' seems the order of the day to extend the scope of the management of learning – though more of the same seems in some cases to mean nothing other than 'more under the same slogan', with little attention to questions of the actual consequences of practices and their justifications.

So it should not surprise readers who discover that what is described and in some ways criticized here as Open Learning (OL) bears little relation to schemes in their own institutions which bear that designation, and so are not subject to these reservations. The use of the term is by no means settled, either in practice or in theory. It gets confused, importantly, with 'teaching at a distance' and 'Distance Education (DE)'. And in the theoretical literature, there is a plethora of other terms, which overlap and often have quite different meanings in different national contexts (such as Australia and the United States) – terms such as external studies, extra-mural studies, home or independent study, off-campus or extended-campus study, and good old 'correspondence education'. It would muddy the waters intolerably (and bore the reader witless) to sift through definitions here. But one other term will be impossible to avoid, and that is 'independent study'. In particular, we shall argue that independent study, in its typical uses, can't be equated with OL.

What follows is not an attempt to stipulate a meaning for OL. Rather, it draws attention to a particular and radical interpretation of it which is, we believe, a useful yardstick against which to compare other developments, the better to discuss their value. Very little of what is currently called OL in Britain is of this radical kind – which stands to higher education almost as deschooling stands, in theory, to schooling. But as an educational ideal, it seems likely to be more and more invoked in the near future to guide and justify managerial innovations.

What then is Open Learning? Like so many terms in newer educational thinking, it lays itself open to capture by definition. Pointless academic games can be played by offering definitions, where the ulterior purpose is not to secure clarity but to secure the institutional dominance of the researcher whose definition 'wins'. In this case, the game is usually played by toying with the word 'open'. Thus it is sometimes asked what it might mean, or more crazily what it 'should' mean, to call a form of education 'open'. But the prior question is why should anyone ask this? What's so special about the word 'open'?

One answer is that the word has acquired a tremendous emotional and ideological power. Extra power is conferred on words when they get linked to important developments, and perhaps the single most potent innovation in higher education since the War was the founding of the Open University (OU). As an institution and an exemplar, which quite rightly commands fierce loyalty from many disparate quarters, the OU itself confers an especial potency on the word used to name it.

Now the Open University, so innocently named, advertises itself as 'open to people, open to places, open to methods and open to ideas'. And here we see immediately that the meaning of the metaphor of 'openness' slips from phrase to phrase. Being 'open' to all people is a different kind of openness from openness to ideas, for instance. The former is a matter of access; the latter is a matter of intellectual curiosity and tolerance – both fine, but not the same thing, with only indirect connections between them. The ringing phrase is excellent for a prospectus, but not for academic analysis. As this example shows, one cannot derive worthwhile definitions of Open Learning by playing semantics with the word 'open'.

Another semantic hitch is that the OU rightly calls itself an institution for Distance Education, suggesting an elision between OL and Distance Education; and indeed many other institutions now seem to advertise their own initiatives based on distance-teaching techniques as OL. Yet, in the literature, the two are sometimes distinguished or even contrasted. The point is that Distance Education is 'open' as to where to study and therefore (in principle) opens higher education to more people. Distance teaching can be used to enhance access. (The question of 'when' to study is subtler. A DE institution like the OU may have its own timetables, for instance. But students are not constrained by 'teaching hours' at least or by whether the doors of the institution are open.)

But this is a different matter from 'openness' in terms of what to learn and how to learn it. Higher education cannot be wholly open in this way. If an institution is to award degrees and diplomas, it must have a say as to what is learnt; and in some cases this may also involve direction as to how it is learnt, the methods involved, if not the time or place or social circumstances. Whilst noting, and applauding, the potential for social openness of DE, we will concentrate on the use of the term 'Open Learning' to designate an intellectually open practice unlike that typical of higher education, and not necessarily conducted 'at a distance' either.

Rather than play the definitions game, it's more illuminating to note the kinds of practices typically associated with a radical practice of OL by many if not by all of its theorists, and to notice the ways in which they hang together as a fairly coherent whole. Those familiar with projects promoting the kinds of practice called 'independent learning' will recognize the same developments, promoted with a different rationale but drawing authority from association with OL.

In its most radical interpretation, OL is seen as maximizing the autonomy of the student and this in turn is interpreted as maximizing or optimizing choice – choosing what to learn and why, the curriculum – as well as where, when and how to learn it. The same autonomy is also taken, in the most radical interpretation, to involve independent learning. By 'independent learning' we mean in the first place learning independently of the activities of any socially present teacher. (We say 'socially present' to include those not physically present. The OU tutor is not physically present but makes herself socially present in communications with students. OU students are not personally independent of their tutors.) That is not to deny that the independent student might consult a teacher. But whether she does so, and why, is up to her.

On the face of it, then, 'Open Learning' looks like not much more than 'going to the library and finding out', the bootstrapping heroism of a hundred working-class heroes in popular or leftish film and fiction from the first half of our century, relating back in effect to the efforts of the Victorian Mechanics' Institutes; and none the worse for that. Learning of this sort involves neither curriculum nor teacher. The institution – if there is one – is only involved as a resource centre. Fully Open Learning does not lead to a qualification because it isn't bound by the requirements of qualifications.

This independent activity, noble as it is, may not seem worth the special attention of educators. But recent developments have given more definite form to the procedures and resources of OL and make it a more plausible model for the future of education. We suggest that five developments in particular have refined the practice into something more distinctive and apparently more powerful than just browsing in a library – though one may be left wondering whether this increased power is real. Most 'theorists' of OL would probably recognize the following as major developments in the practice:

1. the democratization of educational institutions;
2. the proliferation of learning facilitators;
3. the customization of teaching packages;
4. the enhancement of interactivity in teaching texts;
5. the digitization of archives and networking of participants.

First, by 'the democratization of institutions' we have in mind not so much democratic reform in their governance and administration but the opening of institutional doors to ever-wider varieties of students, with increasingly varied purposes and evermore varied interests and expectations. (Of course, it is difficult to democratize in this way without also moving towards a democratized governance. But that's another story.) Not all such democratization promotes OL. The welcome increase in numbers of mature students and of women studying for diplomas and degrees, for instance, is not in itself an increase in numbers in OL. But where democratization takes the form of a proliferation of non-assessed courses and short courses, of open lectures, of inviting local people to help maximize use of resources such as libraries, language labs and meeting rooms, and of courses or events promoting learning in areas which are neither conventionally discipline-bound, nor specific in any vocational direction, there we have forms of democratization which have a claim to be called independent learning under optimal conditions of choice. As such they have a claim on the interest of the Open Learning theorist, however 'Open Learning' might be defined.

In contexts such as these, the role of the learning facilitator is both credible and laudable. It requires knowledge and skill for a student to be able to use effectively the resources of any educational institution, whether material or intellectual – to find and use bibliographies, to optimize use of microfiche versus CD-ROM versus browsing the Net, to understand Dewey and other classification systems, to know how to run self-help groups effectively or find opportunities for attending conferences or seminars, and so on. The fashionable demand for teaching students 'how to learn' is also often thought of as a job for a facilitator. In addition, the learning facilitator may also have an important role in putting appropriate people in contact with each other. ('Oh, you need to talk to

Fred in Earth Sciences.') Importantly, there is a major role in showing people just what is available or possible within any institution. Students in full-time degree work may pick up a lot of this by sheer immersion – yet even they can often miss a lot. And the more democratized institutions become, the less we can presume on such knowledge and skill in occasional users, and the more important the role of the facilitator in providing or developing them. And indeed, this is arguably no job for an academic.

If facilitators are essential to OL, teachers, as we have seen, are marginalized in OL. But this needs qualification. If institutions attempt to maximize the possibilities of choice for the new kind of learner, it does not follow that all such students will seek maximum choice. It does not follow, in particular, that they will all seek complete institutional independence. There is bound to be demand for pre-designed courses of various sorts – requests for teaching with some degree of structure and some degree of guidance from an expert, perhaps with elements of face-to-face teaching, perhaps not. In other words, one element in an Open Learning environment is likely to be a demand-led market in short courses. And to talk of such a market is to posit an expansion in the customization of teaching packages – 'bespoke' courses, tailored to the current demands of specific groups, with no expectation of an extended course life. Such packages may both plunder and reorder existing resources and add new ones. (This possibility is at the heart of current plans for a University of Industry.) The Study Guide, advising students how to use various elements of the package and providing supplementary information where necessary, becomes important here. Modularization of resources is an important prerequisite for such constructions, and this is one way in which a commitment to OL may have implications throughout an institution which is itself more than just an OL institution. The more discretely modularized its certificate courses, the greater its potential for the customization of OL packages.

If learning is rightly thought of as an active rather than passive process, yet the Open Learner is an independent learner, OL packages ideally aim at some degree of interactivity for the student. This can be achieved in print by embedding in teaching texts study advice, in-text questions to prompt and promote reflection or anticipate the direction of argument in the text, Self-Assessment Exercises with answers provided, suggestions for personal project work and further reading and so on. Moreover, a less formal style of presentation can enhance students' identification with the author and engagement with the teaching exercise. A colleague of this writer used to advise authors of such material to write 'as if the reader were sitting with you in your office'. This too may promote active engagement in learning.

In themselves, none of these first four developments entail any use of electronic information technologies at all. All are possible without them and indeed each predates them, sometimes by decades. And certain educational characteristics of this pre-digitized constellation are worthy of notice. On the one hand, all of them can be seen as welcome educational developments in themselves, welcome not only to those committed to Open Learning but also to those involved with formal education, particularly at tertiary level, whether in the conventional mode or 'at a distance' as in the Open University. Obviously we want to see various forms of democratization at this level. Further, there is no reason why university curricula should not become more variegated, providing they are expanded and nothing valuable is lost. And, in a mass system, facilitators are particularly useful. Interactive texts are helpful in any context; and even where curriculum is led by purely academic and disciplinary interests, there can still be a case for customization of courses – for instance, experimentation with new intellectual directions and dimensions, not least of an interdisciplinary kind.

In fact, the UK Open University has been the leading international innovator with regard to the first, second and fourth of these developments (indeed, a misleading picture of the practice of the OU might suggest they were the principal practices of the institution), so in effect much important developmental traffic has actually been from higher education and Distance Education to Open Learning more generally, rather than the other way round. Moreover, and very importantly, some element of Open Learning has for a very long time been an element even in conventional higher education and in fact a highly valued one. It manifests itself more or less obviously in the Oxbridge tutorial system, thesis or dissertation work at many levels (themselves a kind of customization) and in the assumption that a good student will do plenty of 'background reading', more or less undirected and unassessed. A degree that doesn't include such elements confers diminished authority on the student.

But that said, none of these developments are managerially particularly efficient until they are modified and reformed by use of the new information technology. Open Learning practices carry an emphasis on the personal, the individual, the idiosyncratic and the small scale which is not in itself patently cost-effective. Democratization can be costly inasmuch as it means serving more people for longer time. The costs of facilitators need offsetting by cuts in teaching if they are not to be a net expense. Repackaging modules can be expensive if the practice is added on to conventional provision and the design of interactive material is by no means cheap or simple. In themselves, they could never have had any obvious appeal as managerial strategies for solving the problems of mass participation in tertiary education, until the recent explosive dissemination of the new electronic technologies. Only in this new technological context can democratization be absolutely maximized by the opening of electronic gateways to access – access at a distance, or at everyone's mutual convenience (not least, access for the disabled). Low-level facilitation can be electronically mediated, by multimedia packages and by Net or e-mail, enabling facilitators to reach more 'clients' efficiently and to free time either for more sophisticated forms of one-to-one service or for higher-level strategic roles; either way, for increases in educational power. And, patently, new electronic media bear the potential to optimize customization and interactivity with previously unknown ease and effectiveness. A facilitator might be called on by a student to help with customization.

These are the kinds of development in flexibility and efficiency that begin to look not just like useful elements in tertiary education but rather like its potential core, if not actually a substitute for it. Not all learning independent of a teacher need be OL, governed by unfettered choice – there can be such a thing as independent learning that is not under maximal or optimal conditions of choice. In particular, where the learning contributes to following some kind of course or gaining some kind of qualification, then choice will inevitably be restricted, or perhaps rather directed along certain routes. There will be at least a minimal curriculum (this is true even at doctoral level, even though the doctoral 'curriculum' is wholly negotiable) and some form of assessment. Nonetheless, the actual activities of learning might still be partly if not wholly independent of a teacher. In this situation, the learner is personally but not institutionally independent. She can determine 'where, when and how' to study, but not 'what and why', once committed to a degree or other qualification. She is in a very similar situation to the student in Distance Education, even if she is a full-time student at a local institution. (Whether we call such forms of learning 'truly independent' seems to be a fairly pointless quibble.)

And this possibility of managed learning, partly or wholly independent of teachers, makes the managers drool. (It is the informing conception of learning for the proposed University for Industry, for instance.) It also sends teachers off to check their pension arrangements. For a vision of independent learning, leading to a qualification in an institutionally defined context, seems to be the dream of some new theorists of higher education – a dream in which a desiccation of teaching is furthered by allegiance to overtly progressivist (if not progressive) ideals. It raises significant problems.

For we argue that independent learning in conventional higher education gains its value from its place in a broader context of teaching and learning which is not independent learning itself. That is to say, its value inheres in its relation to a different kind of learning. There is a difference between the learning which is a response to teaching and the learning which is not[1]. And the difference is in part ethical or political rather than psychological. But in turn this affects what is actually learnt and how valuable it is. Not least it is relevant to any concern to produce intellectual flexibility in graduates.

Even in the most authoritarian of teaching contexts, what a student or pupil learns depends at least in part on the nature of her motivation. For it is this which directs and moulds her attention and effort. (Even within such schemes as Mastery Learning – an American scheme which has never caught on in Britain much – in which a grasp of a circumscribed field of knowledge or a skill is reinforced to the degree of 100 per cent success, the student may learn much else over and above what she is taught. And this might even interfere with what she is taught. Not least, she might learn that education can be a real bore. Or she may learn that she needn't think.)

How then can we conceptualize motivation in relation to Open Learning on the one hand and to independent learning for qualifications in an institutional context on the other? Philosophers, psychologists and educational researchers typically distinguish between extrinsic and intrinsic forms of motivation. Roughly, the intrinsically motivated student studies for no other reason than for interest in or commitment to the subject matter of her studies. She sees that subject as valuable 'in its own right'. She might think, for instance, that the study of chemistry or philosophy or art history is simply a vital element in any worthwhile human culture, that someone should do it and that she is an appropriate person to do so, both from her own point of view and that of society at large. For the extrinsically motivated student, the knowledge he pursues (how easy it is to gender this distinction!) is not necessarily (though it may be) interesting in itself, but primarily is of interest for its use value – for what he can do with it, the problems he can solve or developments he can devise.

This distinction has, for historical reasons, usually been drawn in connection with conventional patterns of teaching and learning. Yet it usually bumps up against theoretical difficulties, in particular those of giving a meaningful philosophical account of 'value in its own right' and of demonstrating the necessity of such forms of value. But, ironically, the distinction can be particularly simple in the context of Open Learning. And moreover, whereas liberal educationists have usually found something suspect in extrinsic motivation, which seems to lay education open to potentially corrupting economic and political influences, this is not obviously the case for Open Learning.

For in conditions of Open Learning, it is lucidly clear just how one would expect a student to behave, given either of these two forms of motivation. The extrinsically motivated student would browse the possibilities, progressively narrowing his attention onto those sources of knowledge or forms of instruction in skills that promise to give him the cognitive goods that he needs. This is obviously in itself a legitimate use of knowledge. And if the Open Learning context implies that his own activities are purely self-regarding and do not impinge on the Open Learning options of others, then it seems no depredation on the system as a whole. In particular, it leaves the way open on the other hand to the intrinsically motivated student to extend and deepen her grasp of her topic 'for its own sake', accumulating indefinitely large stores of knowledge, indefinitely questioned, critiqued and elaborated[2]. In fact, looked at in this way, Open Learning might begin to look like the answer to all our problems.

But it isn't and it can't be. For whatever the virtues of idiosyncratic bodies of knowledge and expertise, gained informally and validated only by the satisfaction of the learner, society has need also to maintain certain kinds of formalized discourses and literatures and cadres of experts to sustain and enact them. It is also arguable – it is the heart of arguments for Liberal Education – that only immersion in such formalized learning contexts can form in students the *autonomous* motives, dispositions, aims and goals which themselves give point and purpose to their own Open Learning initiatives. The alternative to the student forming her own autonomous outlook is direction, explicit and overt or implicit and covert, by political, economic or in some places religious authorities – a state of affairs quite intolerable in any democracy, and at best of questionable value in an economy of free enterprise. Thus, in countervailing these pressures and empowering the autonomous student, institutionalized education helps build the context necessary for forays into Open

Learning to flourish. Whether or not we use the *methods* of Open Learning, we need also specifically designed courses in particular subjects and disciplines, assessed and leading to accredited qualifications.

And here we get back to the central point of this chapter. As soon as study becomes study structured by curriculum design and leading to some specific qualification, as soon as it becomes independent learning rather than fully Open Learning, the dynamics of intrinsic and extrinsic motivation both change. And this in turn puts independent learning in an institutional context in a quite different light.

Consider first extrinsic motivation. The student who pursues with extrinsic motives a course designed by others inevitably makes various compromises. The course, relevant as it may be in general terms, is necessarily oriented to client groups rather than particular individuals and cannot be guaranteed to give him direct answers to particular problems that exercise him or the specific skills he needs. It is likely, at best, to be only generally or indirectly relevant to those requirements. It may also well include otherwise irrelevant demands on him which he must nonetheless meet if he is to gain the qualification and use it for access to the job in which his knowledge and training can be used. This is a recognized problem in vocational education. But it is not one with any clear solution. If pure relevance is to be the criterion, then Open Learning without accreditation must be the method. But insofar as there is any vocational requirement for the discipline of coursework, then compromises with relevance are inevitable. Courses can be bespoke, but not to specific practical problems.

So what happens in such circumstances to the student's experience of learning? Either he must set aside his original extrinsic motives and acquire an intrinsic interest in the range of things offered him by the course, happy to have his horizons broadened. Or alternatively, and this is very familiar, he takes a purely instrumentalist attitude to the course, jumping through the hoops just to get the qualification. Alistair Morgan has suggested (Morgan, 1993: 35–7) a useful distinction between intrinsic or extrinsic forms of vocational motivation, the former governed by interest in the real demands of a job, the latter by the tiresome necessity of gaining qualifications. I suggest that the only kind of learning appropriate to intrinsic vocational motivation is some form of Open Learning. I also suggest (and I think Morgan agrees) that the kind and quality of learning involved in pursuing pre-defined courses for extrinsic vocational motives is almost inevitably limited, blinkered, inflexible and open to rapid decay and forgetting once the qualification is gained, and not wholly intrinsically useful for the job. As Morgan has found, such students are highly 'cue-oriented', picking up clues from teachers, materials and fellow students as to the necessary minimum they must do and narrowing their perspectives radically to study as little as they need, and as superficially as they need, to gain the qualifications. Where such students do broaden horizons, contrary to expectation, it is reasonable to suppose they have set their extrinsic vocational motives to one side for a time. Generally, extrinsic motivation in the qualification-oriented environment of a ready-designed course tends to lower standards of achievement.

What does this imply for independent learning in such environments? What, indeed, would constitute a course of this kind run on independent learning lines? Here, face-to-face teaching would be replaced by a structured package of materials and activities of the kinds discussed above in relation to Open Learning. (Facilitators might indeed have a role too.) And the demands of such a course will set parameters – limits and goals – on the potentiality for study that Open Learning techniques might otherwise open out. They will define certain avenues of enquiry as peripheral or irrelevant and create a hierarchy of importance amongst whatever is included; indeed that's half the point. This in itself is no loss, providing that there is a teacher involved who can open out in depth what the course curriculum necessarily closes off in breadth. For a course also restricts the time available to study it; so there is no guarantee that students will inevitably pursue in depth, or with any engaged critical sense, those things the course specifies to occupy their time. The teacher is the one who can at least try, and sometimes succeed, in showing the student the value of taking a topic seriously in its own terms and not dismissing or dealing with it superficially in order just to 'secure the grade'. But where there is no teacher, the use of Open Learning methods in the context of designed courses leading to qualifications are almost bound to promote forms of learning which are narrowed, blinkered and closed.

Perhaps we can better understand the mechanisms here if we look at the comparable distortion in the case of intrinsically motivated learning where the learner is nonetheless also abandoned to independence in an institutional context. In this case, there are in fact two possible rationales for such arrangements. Where it is a case of educating large numbers in non-vocational subjects, the learning package is once again the required tool, since standardization of provision has to be the aim. Here, all the problems just noted, where extrinsic learning motives are met with learning packages, are replicated in much the same way. Such packages are ill-adapted to cater to the idiosyncrasies of intrinsic interest. (Attempts have often been made to obviate these problems by writing into such packages invitations and opportunities for the student to stand back, practise, critique, expand or otherwise mull over the offerings. But these rarely succeed very well. Students in such circumstances have vested interests in declining the invitations. Time is short and the stakes are too high.)

However, where course populations are small, and thus the courses uneconomic, there is a managerial temptation to minimize cost by minimizing teaching, putting all the weight of teaching on to assessment, and no doubt minimizing that as well. In such a context, any learning 'package' can become a pretty minimal affair ('Do what you want and we'll mark it!') and the activities of students might seem to approximate much more to genuine Open Learning. There are a few such courses around, but economic pressures imply that we may expect many more in the near future. But while we have only patchy evidence as to what actually happens, common sense indicates that this strategy poses certain dilemmas.

The 'Catch-22' here is that such courses are still intended to lead to accreditation for degree or diplomas. Therefore, the awarding institution, and the department and academics involved, are charged with responsibility to ensure the academic validity of the studies each student has made. An increasing number of course designers face the same problem *in parvo* wherever they want to include an element of project work or short dissertation in a course. Validating boards are typically and rightly wary of complete openness. And the only circumstances in which they typically accept such openness is where the student has a close one-to-one relation with, and guidance from, a tutor – *ex hypothesi* not the situation we are considering here. Otherwise, to ensure academic validity, sets of parameters have to be laid down, sometimes including even a required structure for the final product. And of course, as soon as this is done, we cease to have a genuine exercise in Open Learning. So what, then, do we have?

We still have independent learning, of course. But the constraints will structure the student's activities in highly specific ways, and of course are intended to do so. But what kind of learning is likely to result? Where the course is the student's principal or only experience of a particular sub-discipline or topic, there is necessarily an interest in maximizing the academic 'pay-off' of such work. This interest will be exacerbated the more we come to see such methods used in relation to core areas of disciplines, and not just specialisms. But how would an intelligent student achieve this? Not, surely, by grazing (or should we say browsing?) in happy pastures of indefinite possibility but rather by homing in as accurately as possible on the canonic papers, the best bibliographies, the strongest authorities, in some cases even the 'right' answers. She will want to find the most powerful verbal formulae, the clichés of the field. She will need to construct for herself, as far as she is able, canonic learning experiences that guarantee her the access to the field which no tutor is going to give her in this arrangement. (She will need to do this even when guided by a reading list. For then the pressure is to work out why the list is as it is.)

In sum, if she seeks to optimize the use of her independent time in pursuit of accreditation, her learning experience is likely to be one of a self-imposed academicism, in the pejorative sense. What she will not have the time or emotional security to indulge is her critical sense. She will be too busy constructing and teaching herself what others are no longer giving her. But so what? If others were giving her this canonic learning experience, wouldn't that be academic in the same pejorative way?

Well it could be, of course. But it needn't be. And indeed, one of the best reasons for teaching to a structured curriculum is to provide both a secure structure within which critique can be entertained and pursued and the dialogue with an expert, the teacher, which can provoke critique, help to sharpen it, evaluate the critique (not all critique is sound), and validate critique itself as an important academic activity. Where a course design posits certain texts or ideas as canonic, the student is relieved of any need to demonstrate or establish that canonicity herself. It saves her time. But in doing so, it opens up the space in which critique of canonic work can be broached and moreover accorded its special importance. (Critique of Kant is more important, for instance, than critique of some minor Victorian Idealist.) Thus the proper task of a teacher is to open up a critical study of that canon. Again, what the course design closes off in breadth, the good teacher compensates for by opening up the material in depth. She can do this in the dialogue of the seminar or tutorial. She can also use the freedom of that maligned institution, the lecture, to make public her own doubts, questions, prevarications, countervailing intuitions, disappointments, commitments – all the things which can't so readily go down on the page of a book or journal in black and white, but which may promote critique amongst students by example, the example of the committed expert thinking out loud.

Critique is intrinsically dialogical, a response to doubt and questioning. It involves elements of knowledge no less than skill, but moreover also dispositions informed by normative commitments. None of these are readily or reliably 'picked up' by students working independently. And, *ex hypothesi*, the independent learner is under pressure to marginalize questions, complexities, qualifications, to obviate lacunae, insofar as the pressure on her is fundamentally to assure the paradigm learning experiences for herself – to some degree to reinvent the academic wheel. It takes a teacher to offer the right kind of provocation and upset to demonstrate other possibilities. Thus without the teacher, independent learning in this kind of context is once more not Open Learning but a self-imposed narrowness, risking dogmatism.

The watchwords of current reform are flexibility and quality. And the felt need for extending opportunities for education and training is more than just the ambition to facilitate Open Learning: '... the need for careers to have regular refuelling *through formal or explicit learning* to supplement experience has only recently been accepted' (Hillman, 1996: 3; my italics). Can we have them all? Yes we can. But we can't get them by abandoning institutional study to the processes of independent learning. Open Learning methods pressed to the service of independent learning, and to the achievement of qualifications and accreditation, have the opposite to the intended effect. Learning becomes narrowed and blinkered, liable to rapid decay. It is not just that it is an abuse of language to speak here of flexibility. More importantly, students abandoned to such methods cannot possibly acquire the personal characteristics and cognitive wealth that we need for them if they are to play the role we want in our economic success (never mind the sustenance of our culture or the norms of our society). True flexibility and genuine quality in learning require good teachers. Their contribution is ineradicable.

So where does this leave the computers? To argue for the fundamental role of the teacher is not to argue against the mediation of teaching by computer. The benefits of the use of computers, particularly for Distance Education, are unquestionable (though here too not just anything will do). But in the best uses of such technologies, the teacher is intimately involved, often even in one-to-one, certainly one-to-many, electronic communications.

This has an important implication for cost-saving. On the one hand, it's quite right to suggest that Distance Education can save costs for society at large by enabling students to study part time in their own homes and workplaces. But it's quite wrong to assume that colleges and universities can save costs for themselves by moving into DE. The work time of tutors and lecturers would be redeployed, but it is highly unlikely to be cut. Indeed, the innovation might even call for extra staffing, not least with designers, editors, educational technologists and so on. That said, there can indeed be an extension of power for the teacher. Computer mediated communication can be used to teach students on the other side of the world.

What, though, of the often-vaunted cost-saving virtues of new resource- or learning-centres, often advertised as offering 'Open Learning'? These are generally unlikely to be providing OL in the full sense of the word. In fact, they seem virtually bound, in most cases, to be peddling electronic packages for independent learning, not at all customized to the individual. To all intents and purposes, they are more likely to be providing a kind of 'on-site distance teaching' – distant not geographically, but socially distant from the teacher, if indeed there is anyone who might be called a teacher. The mere presence of the ineluctable facilitator will not mitigate this absence at all. Teaching just isn't her job.

Computer-mediated communication in education must not be identified with the management of learning alone. There are strict limits on what the management of learning has to offer us, and the most important things we need are quite beyond its ambit.

Notes

1. Psychology of learning can obscure the difference by focusing on those processes which are internal to the student, even when discussing learning in groups. But these are never and never could be the whole story about learning.
2. These two pictures presuppose a condition which doesn't yet obtain, of the greater part of human knowledge being readily available electronically. But it isn't 'all out there on the Web' yet, very far from it.

8

Economic Success – How the UfI Will Undermine the Universities' Contribution

On the morning the Government launched its Green Paper on Lifelong Learning, BBC TV Breakfast News included a clip of a middle-aged 'work returnee' whose life had been redeemed through work training undertaken at a computer terminal, in a sort of drop-in centre dedicated to the practice. Fine. The caption for the clip was 'University for Industry – student'. Not so fine – rather problematic, actually. For at the time of showing, the University for Industry (UfI) didn't exist. And for many readers of this book, it may still not exist yet. The student was in fact the wholly notional student of a wholly notional institution. He was an actual example of what such a student *would* be like.

Annoying as this might be, it may seem educationally irrelevant, telling us more about the plummeting standards of TV news coverage than anything else. But it points a deeper irony. If and when the UfI does come into being, the caption 'UfI – student' will still be doubly misleading. For it raises the minimal expectations that the University will have a curriculum and will teach students to that curriculum. But if the UfI eventually takes a form at all similar to that outlined in Josh Hillman's pamphlet *University for Industry* (1996), it will do neither. Rather, the UfI will act as a kind of broker and catalyst, putting students in contact with learning opportunities provided by a galaxy of other institutions, large and small, 'kitemarking' those offerings and proactively encouraging, or even commissioning, perhaps, the creation of new learning opportunities. Inasfar as any teaching is involved, that will be provided by the participating institutions themselves, not the UfI. Not that this should concern those institutions too much, apparently, since Hillman anticipates that there will be little of what we traditionally think of as 'teaching' anyway. But strictly, no student will ever be a student of the UfI, but of somewhere else – if indeed the student of any particular institution at all. As Hillman admits, 'University for Industry' is strictly a misnomer (Hillman, 1996: 6).

These other institutions may take an indefinite variety of forms. Any institution which has something to offer to the project of economic success for the country has a potential role to play – firms and businesses, consultancies, perhaps even voluntary groups, no less than schools or colleges. And it would seem extraordinary to suppose that universities, not least the former polytechnics, should not play an important role. (One of Hillman's examples of interesting current practice is delivered by the University of Sunderland.)

While we wait for firmer proposals and legislation – we are still only at Green Paper stage – it does seem highly likely that Hillman's conception will be largely what we get, and the Green Paper seems to confirm this. It has the double merit, from a New Labour point of view, of being at once both interventionist yet on the face of it very cheap (no campus, no new materials of its own, a minimal and largely non-academic staff). It will avoid the limp-wristed inadequacy of Thatcherite *laissez-faire* but also the expensive *dirigiste* blunders of old Labourism (see Hillman, 1996: Chapter 5). Perhaps most credibly and sexily, it is predicated not on the 'white heat of [old] technology' but the cool glow of the new computer screen – cool, as in Cool Britannia. Multimedia and computer networks may not be the entirety of the envisaged infrastructure of the UfI, but they will be at its sleekly purring heart.

As we argued in the previous chapter, developments in IT are undoubtedly vital to the immediate future of education, in the higher education sector no less – perhaps even more – than anywhere else, and to be welcomed. Certainly they also make possible newly flexible forms of educational organization, in particular new forms of Distance Education which further enhance its support for open access, and these may allow us to avoid many educational failures of our recent national history. But they also open the door to more blunders, and a number of major mistakes are already in sight. The fundamental error, already with us, is an epitome of all that is most dangerous in contemporary educational discourse. While Hillman's proposals are informed by (presumably) sound and necessary economic and management research, there is virtually no *educational* analysis of the potential of the new media at all. As we have already indicated, he avoids all but the most cursory and uncontroversial considerations on curriculum and teaching. And this utter vague-ness is most damaging of all when we turn to consider what contribution university teaching might make to such a project. This is dangerous, since, where the contribution of education to economic success is in question, the UfI may prove to be in some respects the only show in town.

The problem is not, clearly, that universities make no important contri-bution to our economic success already, quite the contrary. Nor is it that they will only be doing so in the post-UfI future inasfar as they contrib-ute to the UfI – that is clearly not in prospect either. But it is easier to point to the direct contribution they make in terms of research, rather than in terms of teaching. For instance, when surveyed as to what they want from a good graduate, employers in business typically ask rather for the skills of good generalists than for specific kinds of education, other than for research jobs. But in the nature of the case, it is difficult to explain just why these general 'skills' are important. (And it's a threat to the home universities that, in a globalized economy, researchers can be gathered in from almost anywhere on earth.)

Insofar as it is concerned with higher education, it is this misty area that the UfI addresses, in which higher education is clearly valued for its impact on the general responsiveness of business in a competitive cli-mate, but for which clear rationales seem to be lacking. To call the UfI 'the only show in town' is to point out that it is only in the context of the UfI that there is any serious policy currently directed to this aspect of the universities' contribution at all. But will its proposals in fact promote an improvement in their usefulness or rather an evasion of serious consid-eration of their role and even erosion of best practice?

The fundamental problem that the UfI poses for the universities is the notion of teaching which Hillman adopts. As we will see, the whole model is implicitly based on the conception of Open Learning discussed in the last chapter, conflating Open Learning with the presumption of open access. Hillman picks out a number of issues which he believes need re-evaluation, not so much in their own right as educational issues, but specifically in relation to the needs addressed by the UfI. Of teach-ing, he says we must reconsider

> the roles of teachers and trainers, becoming as much guides, managers and facilitators of learning as providers of information and knowl-edge; of counsellors giving broader guidance on personal develop-ment and learning goals; and mentors providing role models. (Hillman, 1996; 13)

The need for re-evaluation is justified by the claim that 'Existing arrangements are already under great strain from current demand'. This is an explicitly financial rationale, and we may take it that Hillman is implicitly expecting the universities to make their teaching much cheaper.

But something vital is lost in the conceptions of teaching just mentioned, and what is lost is, on the one hand, fundamental to the role of universities and on the other, never conceivably cheap. The picture of the teacher suggested for higher education is of an academic who may or may not be a researcher, who designs course materials and gives occasional guidance to occasional students, but otherwise never (or at best, increasingly rarely) engages them systematically in dialogue, either in classes, seminars or tutorials or *en masse* in a lecture. As the new cliché has it, she is to be not the 'sage on the stage' but the 'guide on the side'.

The problem here arises in part from a (wilful?) misconception of what traditional academic teachers do. Hillman (like many others) writes as if the role has been simply to provide information and knowledge (see above). It is proposed, quite rightly, that there are better ways of doing this kind of job than by face-to-face teaching, and that academics should have more fruitful things to do with students. But providing information and knowledge has never been their primary teaching task. (The construction of knowledge is rather the role of research.) The pedagogic role of the academic has been essentially to teach students how to think, and how to think in the way appropriate to their discipline or chosen vocation. Telling people the facts of chemistry, public administration, economics or maths, and even making sure they understand and remember them, does not turn a student into a chemist, a public administrator, lawyer or mathematician. Nor is learning how to think a matter of learning how to negotiate the problems in a learning package designed to offer information and knowledge, nor even to 'stimulate reflection' on what the student finds out. (That could mean anything or nothing.) It is fundamentally and essentially an exercise involving dialogue (just as a baby only learns to think if its parents engage it in chatter). It must moreover be real dialogue, not just the notional dialogue of questions in text, however helpful they may be, but of actual to-and-fro response. The dialogue need not be face-to-face: it might involve written or computer-mediated communication instead (as in the Open University, for instance). It can be wholly compatible with the social advantages of learning-at-a-distance. But it has to have a coherent point and purpose and a focus. It has to be more or less systematic and more or less demanding. Anything less is just not a university education and not useful for the things that a university education is useful for – even in the realm of business and industry. Moreover, this intensive interaction cannot be simply one-to-many and cheap. And it's for this reason that we doubt whether universities can or should contribute to the UfI, and fear erosion of their fitness for purpose if they try to do so.

Why does Hillman disregard this project of teaching people to think and the special (but not at all unique) role that higher education plays in it? Once again, we are up against the irony of an anti-progressivist culture of educational policy that nonetheless takes progressivist ideals and practices as received educational wisdom. (Open Learning, after all, is a manifestation of educational progressivism.) Yet such progressivist ideals sit uneasily with even the most liberal interpretation of higher education, as we indicated in Chapter 7. And the first educational failure of Hillman's analysis, which must shout from the page to any educationist who reads it, and which flows from this naïve and misplaced progressivism, is the almost complete elision of education and training.

Traditionally educationists have seen these two practices as related but significantly different. In a democracy, education is valued for constructing and expanding the autonomy of the student or pupil, intellectually, culturally, morally, politically, indeed in matters of religion too. A democratic citizen requires education. Thus, education must be centrally concerned with furthering not merely knowledge but understanding, and understanding of a wide range of issues. And education, either in a particular subject or discipline or in a vocation or profession, must be centrally concerned both with predicating that study as intrinsically open to further elaboration, both in breadth and depth, and also with equipping the student or pupil to carry on learning in such ways once their formal education is complete (or at least temporarily adequate).

The aims of training are paradigmatically specific and closed. This is no scandal (such as rote learning, for instance, is often thought to be), for the aims of training are not an alternative to education but its complement. We need training because there are certain kinds of activity, knowledge or task for which cut-and-dried criteria of competence can be specified, and such that optimum performance is the value that accrues to them rather than any indefinite potential for development. Sometimes those tasks have a utilitarian value quite unconnected with education. Sometimes their value is to make education itself easier or more fruitful to pursue. Either way, training has its own importance.

(There is an anomaly of usage here. We often talk about training in a much more open-ended way than this. Training a nurse or a teacher, for instance, is not typically thought of as so narrowly focused an affair, and should indeed involve bringing them to a sophisticated degree of flexibility and initiative. In part, use of the word 'training' is a historical hangover from days when such vocations were actually seen in much more limited terms. While we may sometimes still use the phrase 'teacher training', it's actually the education of teachers that we really have in mind. The same goes, for instance, for nurses.)

But the distinction between training and education remains of fundamental importance to a project such as the UfI. Patently, for instance, the roles of teachers and trainers are different (even where one person might do both), and the ways in which either might be developed in the new information technology context are also different. Moreover, if one thing conventionally sets higher education apart from the rest of education, it is its virtually exclusive focus on education rather than training; so that any possible relations between universities and the UfI depend on a clear appreciation of some economic role in the UfI's mission for education proper, as opposed to training. Yet nowhere in either Hillman's pamphlet or the Green Paper is the distinction seriously considered. And there are reasons for this.

The first is that the UfI is to be a student-centred, demand-led institution. In repudiating the temptations of *dirigisme*, of any kind of national plan for an adult vocational curriculum, Hillman writes: 'While adults frequently need guidance and advice [student support], they are usually better placed themselves to assess what they need than anyone else' (Hillman, 1996: 33). (Echoes of Baroness Thatcher's dogma against taxation – that the individual is the one who best knows how to spend his own money.) But if we accept this, it seems to follow that the employee as an individual is also the one who knows best whether she needs training rather than further education or indeed higher education, or vice versa (a conclusion which is surely palpably implausible from the moment it is stated – do employers not have a valid view?). In that case, a demand-led system cannot properly draw the distinction but must cater to both without discrimination. Hillman does not say this explicitly. But it is hard otherwise to make sense of this elision.

The second reason is Hillman's inattention to distinctions (admittedly tiresome) such as those of the last chapter; in particular, the distinction between Distance Education, open access and Open Learning. DE and OL may be, and largely both are, characterized by open access, and a good thing too. They may also share the same kinds of institution, modes and media of transmission, which, as we have noted, are of much interest to Hillman. But he slides into the assumption that there are no educational differences: in particular, no pedagogic differences in the role and intensity of involvement of teachers. Hillman refers indiscriminately to the roles of Distance Education in vocational training on the one hand and in vocational education on the other, as if they could and should be more or less homogeneous – as if the distinction between the two were illusory. In particular, he implicitly assumes that Distance Education methods in higher education are no different from those appropriate to Open Learning.

And it's worth pointing to an ideological position which, if not explicitly Hillman's, makes this elision politically acceptable to many. Training has indeed been widely thought of in the past as a cognitively inferior practice, appropriate to socially inferior activities, so that insistence on drawing the distinction with education is readily seen as poisonously élitist. (The failures of the post-1944 bipartite educational system are closely related to this, grounded in the fantasy that a 'technical' education for the majority could achieve 'parity of esteem' with the academic education of the grammar school minority.) Add to that the undeniable failures of training in this country over a very long period of time, and it may easily come to seem that the distinction is positively dangerous to maintain, no less than offensive.

But notwithstanding these reasons, the failure to draw the distinction remains not just dangerous but puzzling. For if we are to go for a demand-led system, how do we sustain the insistence of Hillman and others, from which we do not in the least demur, that a rethinking of the role of all sectors of education in our economic success is so very urgent? If the individual is to be the one who decides what she needs, what's to stop her saying that she needs not very much? Or only low-level inputs, irrelevancies or a narrow minimum? In particular, if the system is to be demand-led, what guarantees the more than marginal or occasional relevance of higher education to this national project?

It is no answer here to insist, as Hillman does, more than once, that there is a huge pool of 'latent demand' just waiting to be unstoppered by the appropriate supply, so the questions are academic. That may be the case, although the claim needs treating with caution. The more fundamental question concerns the composition of the demand. And the pretence that we just can't tell what this will or should be is belied by policy makers like Hillman himself, who see these needs even though, *ex hypothesi,* potential students have not yet had the chance to manifest their demand in the appropriate markets. The whole project is predicated on perceptions of need quite other than any communicated by market choice. And indeed, if this were not so, there'd be no rationale for calls such as Hillman's to expand, open up and invigorate the 'learning market'. But why, if there is some perceived rationale, is there no curriculum? Why is the prospect of such a curriculum dismissively equated with *dirigisme*? Why in particular is there no distinction drawn between needs for training and for education, the most basic curricular distinction of all? We've seen factors (such as intellectual and social snobbery) which vitiate the attempt to make the distinction. But are they good justifications for ignoring it?

The diffidence in defining a 'curriculum' is in part a corollary of the non-educational nature of the research that informs proposals like Hillman's. The belief that we need vastly improved education and training is grounded principally on comparative statistics that draw rough correlations between indices of education and training and of economic success across the international spectrum. So, for instance, numbers of young adults still in full-time and particularly higher education, levels of certificated attainment, percentage of gross domestic product (GDP) devoted to education and so on all correlate positively with levels of output, technological advantage, levels of employment and unemployment and, most of all, size of GDP. (Though it should be noted that, at the time of writing, such correlations are themselves being put in question again: see Robinson, 1998).

Now of course, research like this can tell us very loudly *that* we need much improved provision. But it can't tell us why. It can't show us just *how* the educational factors impinge on the results. And nor, therefore, does it show us just how different forms of educational provision impinge on economic success, for all the intuitive obviousness of the connection. Nor is it enough just to propose that we copy the distribution of various forms of education found abroad. Their success in turn depends at least in part on their consonance with their own different institutional, social and cultural contexts and histories. Even if we wish to imitate, we will almost certainly have to modify as well; and to do so successfully requires understanding of educational mechanisms – something economic and management research alone cannot give us. A curriculum designer, on the other hand, would start from this important question 'Why?' Her question would be, 'What knowledge do we need (and for whom)? And what do we need it for?'

It is not *dirigisme* to ask such questions. Not all initiatives by central government can be classed as such – after all, the UfI itself would be a central initiative. *Dirigisme* is not a matter of a central agency having or even acting on a view of its own. It is the situation in which the central view is treated as exhaustively and uniquely relevant. To avoid *dirigisme*, central agencies need not retreat to a vapid agnosticism. They may still ask pointed and apposite questions. And answering these questions, as we shall show, is a precondition of coming to any intelligent conclusions about the kinds of provision we need, *dirigiste* or otherwise. The question which particularly concerns us here is whether there is some specific role for higher education.

With the distinction between education and training in mind, a first refinement of these questions could usefully be to ask whether the knowledge needs of the economy are specific or general. What is our problem? Is it that businesses and other bodies lack personnel with specific abilities relevant to specific activities within their organization? Or is it that the economy at large needs a workforce better educated in skills or forms of knowledge which might themselves have little obvious direct or immediate relevance to specifiable jobs, yet nonetheless raise the level of performance of the system as a whole? The question is vital. The latter proposition entails a role for higher education in economic development. The former arguably does not.

If the problem is simply that businesses lack people with specific skill or knowledge, then the vast diversity of such demands seems to imply that the responsibility for doing something lies largely with those businesses themselves. Not even universities and colleges (and certainly not schools) can cater to such specialized heterogeneity. It might be that businesses themselves could and should provide better education and training from their own resources of knowledge and understanding. If that were so, arguably government need only arrange systems of sticks and carrots to encourage this. (Let's admit that this has proven consistently difficult, though – consider the unhappy history of some of the TECs.)

But it might alternatively be the case that many businesses lack the information, skill or knowledge that they need to do the training job themselves. (It might in fact be businesses that need to be taught how to train, as much or more than their employees need to learn how to learn.) That would indeed argue for a better-developed and co-ordinated network of contacts to put firms seeking this help in touch with potential providers. The Internet would obviously be an appropriate and important tool here, but such provision would still stop a long way short of what even is proposed for the UfI. Neither this nor the previous scenario suggests any need or point in employees cruising shopping centres on their day off, to track down a training centre providing access to some ill-defined training opportunity, which might or might not be relevant to some work need their employers had neither specified nor attempted to cater for themselves. Only a minimal kind of scheme would be necessary. Here there would be no case for any government sponsored curriculum development and the form of assisted market provision proposed for the UfI would be appropriate. It would indeed entail learning on demand, but the demand of the employer, and for the employer, not of or for the employee. And it would probably involve higher education very little, if at all.

But it seems obvious that this is not what any proponents of a University for Industry have in mind, however vague their proposals might be. So what more sophisticated needs might justify such provision?

The Green Paper on Lifelong Learning says this with regard to the UfI:

> we will need to provide better quality goods and services, high added value and productivity, and be able to use technology to the full. This will require investment in the skills and abilities of management and workforce alike....

Clearly, it conceives the knowledge requirements dictated by such needs as skills (or in some cases as discrete bodies of knowledge, such as the naming of parts of a complex machine or competence in a limited class of mathematical computations). It identifies its immediate educational priorities as improving

- basic skills;
- information technology skills;
- the management of small and medium sized businesses;
- skill needs in specific industries and services.

This is actually not a list of kinds of skill, it should be noticed, but of areas and levels of activity in which a range of skills, not here identified, are called for. If these were the whole remit of the UfI, it would be hard to see how higher education might be involved at all. But these are in fact only priorities. Their interest to us lies in the fact that in the literature, skills in these areas are typically conceived as 'generic' or 'transferable' skills. It is taken for granted that there is a significant corpus of skills or bodies of knowledge whose attainment facilitates performance in a range of significantly disparate activities, so that learning them makes the employee more readily able to switch to a different job or different kind of work – which makes him or her more flexible as an employee.

But would faith in generic skills itself justify the project of a system at all resembling Hillman's? And would higher education have a role in such a system? Not on this basis alone, for a further and essentially pedagogic consideration would make the difference. The question would arise first whether generic skills could be taught independently of learning any particular job, task or activity. There are reasons to doubt it. Philosophically, to have a skill is nothing other than to be able to perform some activity skilfully, that is, to meet certain standards in connection with the activity. Being competent is not a matter of having something-like 'competence' (*pace* the fantasies of the National Council for Vocational Qualifications) bolted on to what one does, but simply to be able to do the one thing in a certain way. This entails that skills can't be acquired independently of learning particular activities – to think otherwise is to see them like the grin on a Cheshire cat. But no cat, no grin; no activity, no skill. At the very least, we can say that job training is necessary to the acquisition of job-related skill, whether that skill is generic or transferable or not.

Yet if that is so, then the acquisition of generic skills would have to be not just married to, but actually an aspect of, training in the workplace. One could only acquire generic skills in doing specific jobs. And then the vision of a motivated workforce seeking out further training in generic skills outside their own working lives as an investment in the future would remain futile. Moreover, the more such generic skills someone wanted to acquire, the greater the variety of actual work experiences he or she would have to have. And the acquisition of this flexibility would not be straightforwardly an asset for acquiring wide experience; on the contrary, wide experience would itself be a precondition of acquiring flexibility itself. This is obviously not a project in which higher education might play any significant part.

More promisingly for finding a role for higher education, it might be suggested that even if specific job experience were necessary to acquire generic skill, it still would not be sufficient. David Blunkett's words in his foreword to the Green Paper are thus more encouraging for job-independent learning:

> This Green Paper sets out for consultation how learning throughout life will build human capital by encouraging the acquisition of knowledge and skills and emphasizing creativity and imagination. The fos-

tering of an enquiring mind and the love of learning are essential to our future success.

There is some plausibility in the suggestion that the acquisition of generic skills themselves requires a development of certain more advanced intellectual capacities, including perhaps also the ability to reflect upon the nature of what one is learning to do. (Reference to Donald Schön's well-known notion of the 'reflective practitioner' is never far away in these discussions.) But notice two things here. First, this does not sidestep the point just made, that there would have still to be actual training in skills, and this would still have to be work-based. But secondly, insofar as the acquisition of generic skills is thought to be enhanced by something further, by more general intellectual talents and positive attitudes to education, then that already argues for some kind of education rather than just training and for an embryonic curriculum of the very kind Hillman wishes to avoid. One would surely be talking here of specifiable but general and open-ended intellectual qualities (imagination, creativity, good judgement, sympathetic insight) which of their very nature require the open-endedness of education to cultivate them, not the closed routines of training. In other words, one would be thinking in terms of a collection of courses – in terms, that is, of a curriculum. These courses would be appropriate not to on-the-job training but to independent study.

And indeed, quite inconsistently, Hillman himself in effect outlines some such curriculum in passing:

> lifelong learning must start at school with a broad and solid foundation including 'learning to learn'… It will be particularly important for people to… master such key skills as communication, independent learning, navigation of information sources, team working, problem-posing and problem-solving and an understanding of wider work processes and systems. (Hillman, 1996: 3)

The specifics of this embryonic curriculum are pretty dubious. Nonetheless, one might begin to glimpse a role for higher education in this 'hidden curriculum': a role, perhaps, in giving people the intellectual equipment to become more sophisticated practitioners in appropriate ways and in respect of a variety of aspects of their work[1].

But is this kind of provision genuinely appropriate for economic success? The discourse of the 1990s on the supposed need for generic skills in the workforce is predicated on a particular prognosis for industry in the developed (and developing) world. The picture informing calls for flexibility is one in which technology evolves in a series of Kuhnian hiccups. Thomas Kuhn (1962) proposed a picture of the evolution of science in terms not of a linear and gradual development, but of a series of stepwise revolutions or paradigm shifts, in which one way of doing some particular specialism is suddenly overthrown and some radically distinct practice put in its place. Applying such a picture to the likely evolution of technology yields a prognosis for an economy in which workers can expect to have to unlearn or discard one set of skills or knowledge and acquire another, quite different, not once but several times in a career. Flexibility, the ability to jump around like this, can be conceived in two ways. Either it is nothing other than the political docility to accept this utter disruption, not just of one's life but of one's work-moulded identity. Or, more positively, it is a personality trait that enables one to move around because one is rich in transferable skills, which are intellectual benefits in their own right.

But as we have noted in Chapter 3 and elsewhere in this book, arguably there are no such skills. For instance, 'communications skills' sound helpfully general. But they are indeed far too general. What is there in common between the communication skills needed by a nurse running a self-help group for expectant mothers, a shop-floor manager and an accountant communicating with lawyers? What skills of problem-posing are shared by an industrial middle manager, a systems analyst or a local arts administrator? In short, what relevance could even a curriculum for independent study have to any demand for generic skills, any more than one predicated on specific skills needs in particular industries? Any input from higher education into specific work contexts would have to be predicated on much tighter and contractually specific links between a business and a university than is envisaged in the Green Paper or for the UfI.

Yet calls for flexibility still seem intuitively reasonable. Might it not be, then, that flexibility has been wrongly conceived? We suggest this is so, and that the needs picked out in the Green Paper (above) call for a different kind of flexibility themselves. Perhaps the flexibility which matters most is not flexibility in changing jobs or careers, but flexibility within one's career? For there is no clear reason to suppose that Kuhnian paradigm shifts will occur as radically or as often as we currently are encouraged to suppose, and even less reason to expect them to happen concurrently in diverse fields of industry. A shift in computing technology, for instance, may entail a shift in car production. But it would hardly entail the demise of car production altogether.

If we are not perhaps so likely to need to comprehensively re-make ourselves as managerial fashion currently proposes, modern markets and technologies nonetheless call for flexibility for other reasons. It is often said that the newer industries are not resource-based so much as knowledge-based. But what does this mean? It is much more than the mere idea that resources are now as often intellectual as material. It also involves the insight that knowledge, unlike skills (which may also be intellectual), has a potential for expansion, elaboration in depth as well as breadth, revision and refinement, and that it also involves typically an appreciation of where the lacunae, inadequacies or plain errors of a body of knowledge lie – that knowledge involves understanding. It further proposes that growth for a company increasingly presupposes furthering basic research and not just applied refinements of a given technology. (As Cantwell and others have pointed out (Cantwell, 1995), those companies best at using the research of others are those who put most into doing their own research as well.) And an important corollary is that forms of organization and work practices need often to change in order to accommodate new applications of new knowledge. A knowledge-based industry does not just raise its stake in research, it is continually open to re-formation and realignment in the light of research findings, for both management and staff.

But it is not just adaptation to changes in the knowledge base that require flexibility in the successful enterprise. New uses of given knowledge will also do so. For instance, in the post-Fordist company, as it is often pointed out, novel variations in demand might best be met by alterations in short production runs changes which are themselves less than radical Kuhnian shifts, but nonetheless unpredictable and calling for deep understanding of the basic nature of the product. Product innovation too may not so much draw on a new body of knowledge as involve a creative reuse of what is already known. But the knowledge presupposed here needs the kind of flexible openness that the skills model cannot provide. And even without significant innovation or market changes, the successful company always sees before it a range of directions in which it may gradually evolve. Even to foresee and understand these directions, never mind to choose between them, also requires the depth and flexibility of understanding of which we are talking.

Thus, continued strong performance in the same job may require intellectual flexibility, no less than the ability to switch to something new when the growth of knowledge requires it. But the flexibility here is not a matter of skill. *Pace* the delusive redefinitions of the National Council for Vocational Qualifications, knowledge just cannot be reconceived as a skill. It isn't a more or less adaptable response to varying situations of the same kind (like skilfully adjusting a tennis shot to a ball). A flexible grasp of a body of knowledge is the ability, not only to traverse it and map it and to criticize its inadequacies, but also to know how to marry one body of knowledge to another or to explore its *terra incognita*. But what matters for us here is not merely whether knowledge can be classified as skill, but the fact that it requires a quite different pedagogical approach.

What we have just outlined is not a case for improving generic, and by extension specific, skills. As we have seen, it does not have to do with skills at all but with knowledge and understanding. In particular, it has to do with the extension of perspectives, the refinement of judgement and its grounding, its stimulus to imagination and creativity which only induction into a corpus of knowledge can bring. In all these respects, it is a case for the intellectual development of a workforce beyond the immediate and obvious demands of its current tasks – not least, the better to see what other tasks demand its attention. So unlike the development of generic skills, this is not to be linked to training; and in that respect it is potentially appropriate for the involvement of higher education.

But this is no case for subsuming higher education under the kinds of pedagogic arrangement foreseen for the Ufl. The intellectual developments called for all involve that systematic challenge to the learner that is typical of higher education. Systematic challenge entails a curriculum. Indeed, these high level intellectual talents can no more be developed *in vacuo* than generic skills. And whatever knowledge base informs them in any particular case needs to be specified. But as we saw in the previous chapter, this in turn entails the intervention of a teacher to secure the depth of learning which gives it value, in default of the indefinite breadth possible in Open Learning. The upshot is that insofar as higher education has a serious contribution to make to the education of the workforce, it cannot but involve precisely that intensive mode of teaching which is just not captured at all by the model of 'the guide on the side' – the teacher as facilitator, counsellor, mentor or manager of learning. It is the teacher not as 'sage on the stage' but as interlocutor, provocateur, protagonist and authority – and as much more than purveyor of information.

All of this, as we have seen, can be provided through the open access offered by Distance Education and indeed can be computer-mediated.

But none of it is cheap. It is just not possible to optimize the impact of higher education on business by trivializing its teaching methods to enhance access or by substituting Open Learning. Once the gains of Distance Education are secured, access needs to be enlarged by enhancing academics' skills in the traditional role and expanding the teaching force. There is no other way.

We have not produced here some effete and élitist rationale for abstracting the universities from the project of national economic progress. If anything, we have done the opposite, and tried to show exactly how and why they have an important role. But we believe we have also indicated that this role cannot be performed on the cheap and that the proper contribution of the universities simply cannot possibly be subsumed under the aegis of the University for Industry. Count us out, please.

Notes

1. Ron Barnett has argued for the importance of reflective practice in higher education (Barnett, 1992).

9

A Music Discourse

It is important to remember how rich teaching and learning in higher education can be: how rewarding and, to use one of Dearing's own phrases (1.1.), life-enhancing, not only for the student but also for the teacher. As university life threatens to become more and more a series of impersonal modules and hours in front of the computer screen we need such reminders as we can find. There are things which are in danger of being lost. We hope that what follows is recognizable; if it sounds old-fashioned in places, as it surely will to some, that alone should not condemn it.

An academic (lecturer, teacher, tutor, call him what you will: we refer to him as T, and accept from the beginning that there is a gender issue here) has found time for a walk beyond the confines of the campus. He is contemplating writing a research paper, perhaps anxious about his standing in the forthcoming Research Assessment Exercise; he might equally be playing truant from a committee. His motivation is relevant here, and is touched on later in this chapter. The scene might provoke envy on the part of those from other walks of life, but it is unusual for T to be away from his desk or the lecture-room. Anyway, as we have suggested he may have things on his mind that would mitigate any envy.

As he walks he becomes aware that one of his students, S, a promising and pleasant young man, is coming towards him. At five yards' distance a kind of rapport or complicity seems to form in the space between them: at any rate, neither seems able to pass by with merely a nod and a smile. Perhaps each has needs to be met here. T is the first to speak.

'Hello, S. Where have you been, and where are you off to now?'

('Where have you been?' 'Where are you coming from?' If we are to make any real contact with people we do need to know where they are coming from, as the phrase has it; accordingly we told the reader in the introduction something about where we, the authors of this book, come from. A true story, from one of our colleagues: a lecturer has called in to see him a first-year student who has failed to hand in an assignment – a common enough occurrence. The young man apologizes and explains that he really isn't sure that university is for him. And there the matter might end, with a warning perhaps and a rearranged deadline. But where was this student coming from? A few minutes' gentle exploration revealed that this student came from one of the major public schools, and had spent his gap year in South America. It seemed to emerge that whereas university is the promised land for many students, the time of their lives, for this man it came as an anticlimax. He seemed to find this insight helpful, saying as he left 'Perhaps it isn't just that there's something wrong with my head, then.' Apparently his university career continues, bumpily. Note that it does take *time* to find out quite where people are coming from.)

S explains where he has been. He spent the morning in Professor L's lecture. Professor L is something of a star. He holds a number of visiting professorships elsewhere, and catty remarks are sometimes made about how students are lucky to find him on campus, or they can always catch him on Channel 4 where his series about human language is currently being repeated. This probably explains the cattiness, as does the fact that his courses are extremely popular and require the use of the university's largest lecture theatre, with closed-circuit television for the overspill. He runs the two weekly lectures of S's module end-on, on the reasonable grounds that this is economical use of his time, and of the students'. This way he can spend three days a week writing in his country cottage, and they can put in concentrated effort on the study pack – well-designed and well-structured – that accompanies the course. The large number of students involved unfortunately makes seminars or tutorials quite impossible.

It is not easy to say quite what this particular course or module that S follows is about. It is called 'Communication Skills 237', and is a second-year elective which, according to the Faculty Handbook, 'extends the ideas of the first-year module 'Introduction to Communication Skills 115'. It takes a thematic approach to the nature of human communication and at the same time helps students develop their own practical communication skills over a range of genres and styles. Now T has always found Professor L and his ideas intriguing and slightly worrying in about equal measure. They touch obliquely on some of his own interests, so a conversation with a bright young man who has just been to L's lecture presents the opportunity for T to 'think aloud' and clarify his own thoughts, as well as welcome diversion from gloomy contemplation of Research Assessment (T, it has to be said, does not write much, and does not broadcast at all). S may learn something from the conversation, but T does not engage him with any direct pedagogical intention.

'A good lecture, this morning's?' T asks, cautiously.

'I'd love to go over it with you, but I know you're busy', says S.

T bites back the remark he feels inclined to make, which would be along the lines that neither busyness nor business are doing the academic life a lot of good. Teachers are seldom mentioned in the educational press, he sometimes observes, without the sobriquet 'busy' attached to them: as if buzzing around, probably with files and checklists under your arm, scurrying from meeting to meeting, somehow justified your existence. But all he says is a measured 'Some things are more important than being busy'.

S is more than ready to talk about the morning's lecture, which has caught his interest to a high degree. It concerned personal relationships, and the possibility of using various devices, in speech, writing and body language, to convey a sense of reliability, to inspire trust, even personal loyalty and affection. L traced the history of 'effective writing' from the Greek sophists (much misrepresented, apparently), through Roman rhetoric and Macchiavelli right up to modern practice in business and commerce. S has been much taken with something L brought out, as a valuable and rather special secret, to share with his audience. It seems that there is an acronym, SPACED, the trusty tool of those who make proposals and write tenders. It stands for Security, Performance, Appearance, Convenient, Economical, Durable. S has been rather guiltily wondering whether he could practise the technique somehow on that attractive brunette who sits in the second row.

'Security – you start by showing you're a safe bet, you see', he explains. 'You've got a track record, you aren't going to let them down. Then you go on to the other points one by one. Performance means you show how you'll bring about actual results and enhance the performance of the organization you're tendering to. Appearance means you spell out how the company's image will be improved, or if the outcome is some kind of report you tell them what an attractively produced document it will be, one they will be proud to show to their business associates. You finish up by demonstrating that your way of doing it will be particularly convenient for your client, for example it won't disrupt their everyday business. And you're good value for money, and the effects you achieve won't disappear overnight. It seems that this approach is successful over an enormous range of areas. You tell people what they want to hear, even if they don't know that's what they want to hear. There are several really interesting examples in... in – '

'In the study pack which I see you are carrying. Once students used to bring their Vergil or Wordsworth to read out here, but we move with the times. Why don't we sit down and have a look at it, since it has inspired you so much? We can find somewhere along the river here.'

'It is lovely at this time of year. Mind you don't get your feet wet!'

'Where would be the best place to sit, I wonder?'

'There's a tree with some shade, if you don't mind sitting on the grass.'

'I think I could manage that, even at my age!'

'Someone was telling me that you can swim from here down to the lock and back in an hour. They say students used to do it in the old days for a wager. Is that true, do you know?'

'I've heard that story too. If they did they were certainly risking their lives, because there are strong currents further down that can pull you over the weir. But you were going to tell me more about this morning's lecture.'

(Whatever is going on here? If this is higher education, it doesn't seem to be very efficient – a luxurious staff–student ratio, and some pointless chit-chat about grass and rivers. Still, you can see how it might be interesting to have a lecturer all to yourself for once, and this one seems friendly enough even to step out of role, to the extent of a mild joke about his age. Walking, sitting, minding you don't get your feet wet – perhaps there is just a hint of the 'embodied' nature of learning we referred to in Chapter 5. And it's sensible enough of T to move the conversation on from that undergraduate stuff about swims and wagers. Important to show that student folk-tales aren't an enduringly interesting topic of conversation.)

'What's always great about L's lectures is that they're terrifically well-structured. He starts by telling you exactly what you are going to get out of it, and then he goes over the key points again at the end and reminds you of what you know now or what you can do now that you couldn't do at the start of the lecture. Today he was showing how teaching is a kind of effective communication. It's another way of persuading people to take your ideas on board. The Greek sophists were teachers, and rhetoric is a form of persuasion. That's how we got onto SPACED and what L calls Effective Management English.'

'A lot of interesting ideas there, certainly. And what could you do by the end of the lecture that you couldn't do before? How exactly will these ideas be practically helpful to you?'

'Well suppose – silly example, really – but suppose you knew a girl reasonably well in a casual sort of way, but you wanted to persuade her it was worth taking the relationship onto a different level, and you couldn't think of how to say it face to face, or you were too embarrassed. You could write to her, setting out the advantages, so to speak.'

'Selling yourself, in a manner of speaking.'

'In a manner of speaking, yes. Look, it's only realistic that women want to go out with men who've got something going for them rather than men who haven't.'

'Oh, I'm sure you're right. But I wonder what such a letter would look like.'

'Actually, I've had a go at one. It's one of the set exercises in the study pack, you see. It's not very good, what I've written.'

'I never knew anyone give me an essay worth reading who didn't say that! I'd love to read what you've written, or rather hear you read it. Without my glasses I don't think I could cope with your handwriting, or anyone else's!'

'All right, then. Here goes. I'll leave out the 'dear so-and-so' stuff. 'I think you know my situation. I have always enjoyed stable relationships in the past, and people have found me reliable. The relationship would be one that would help you to do the kinds of things you want to do – '

'Ah. It would enhance her performance.'

'Sort of. ' – and, being a stable relationship, it would give you the kind of emotional security that your university studies need. We'd look good together. I don't have any inconvenient baggage, such as children from a previous relationship' – you're supposed to put it all positively, but I couldn't think of a way of doing it with that bit – 'and, as for the financial side of things – '

'"I can listen no longer in silence. I must speak to you by such means as are within my reach."'

'I'm sorry?'

'"I can listen no longer in silence. I must speak to you by such means as are within my reach. You pierce my soul." Don't worry, I'm quoting from Jane Austen. From *Persuasion*, appropriately enough in view of the fact that we've been talking about persuasion and rhetoric. You know, your letter is rather good. It's a splendid example of its type. It shows how language can be used as a means to an end. But language – communication, if you like – doesn't always work like that, even where a man is writing to a woman he loves.'

'How does it work, then?'

'It's not easy to explain in a few words. I doubt if I shall be able to manage a neat summary of the key points, and I've omitted to bring my overhead projector out here with me! But if you have the time we could do some exploring together. I happen to have a copy of *Persuasion* with me, since I'm thinking of writing something about Jane Austen. In fact that was why I came out here for a walk. Since we became the Department of Communications – we were the Department of English Literature once, you know – I find that I feel guilty about reading Jane Austen in my room.'

'Yet if I understand you right you think Jane Austen has something to teach us about communication. And I do have time, and I'd love to hear why people make such a fuss about Jane Austen! I saw the film of *Sense and Sensibility*, which was quite fun.'

'Perhaps the best thing would be to read a passage together. Jane Austen's letters are always very interesting. I mean the ones she has her characters write to each other. In *Persuasion* a character called Frederick Wentworth writes to Anne Elliott. He is, as we would say now, in love with her, but he is uncertain of how she feels towards him. He has overheard some remarks she has made to others, which give him some hope. Since I only have one copy, could you read this passage aloud for us both?'

'I'll do my best. I hope I shall do it justice.

"I can listen no longer in silence. I must speak to you by such means as are within my reach. You pierce my soul. I am half agony, half hope. Tell me not that I am too late, that such precious feelings are gone forever. I offer myself to you again with a heart even more your own than when you almost broke it eight years and a half ago. Dare not say that man forgets sooner than woman, that his love has an earlier death. I have loved none but you. Unjust I may have been, weak and resentful I have been, but never inconstant. You alone have brought me to Bath. For you alone I think and plan. – Have you not seen this? Can you fail to have understood my wishes? – I had not waited even these ten days, could I have read your feelings, as I think you must have penetrated mine. I can hardly write. I am every instant hearing something which overpowers me. You sink your voice, but I can distinguish the tones of that voice, when they would be lost on others. – Too good, too excellent creature! You do us justice indeed. You do believe that there is true attachment and constancy among men. Believe it to be most fervent, most undeviating in

F.W.

"I must go, uncertain of my fate; but I shall return hither, or follow your party, as soon as possible. A word, a look will be enough to decide whether I enter your father's house this evening, or never."

'Yes, it's impressive, isn't it. I can see how a woman receiving this would be convinced of the man's force of feeling. The ending's certainly dramatic: "whether I enter your father's house this evening, or never." A bit Freudian, too.'

'Now what I want to ask, S, is the following question. "If this is an impressive piece of communication, what kind of communicating is taking place? What is Jane Austen telling us about effective communication, if you like?"'

'I'm not at all sure I understand what you're getting at.'

'Compare it with your study-pack exercise, the letter setting out your advantages and benefits. I don't mean to be over-critical, because I know it was only a first draft and something in your tone of voice when you read it suggested your heart wasn't in it. But communication there was one-way, wasn't it? It was your words for her eyes, your voice for her ears, meant to bring about a result almost as starkly as when someone on the field over there shouted "duck!" to the girl in the flight-path of the football.'

'I'm not clear if this is the kind of thing you mean, but I did notice the letter started with him talking of listening, which was odd when he was, as it were, doing the talking.'

'Yes, listening and not listening, because he says he can listen no longer.'

'But he can "listen no longer in silence". That doesn't mean that he isn't listening, only that he can't do it without wanting to say something.'

'Very good. So he is listening, not listening and listening. And then he does speak, doesn't he?'

'He says he *must* speak, which isn't the speaking so much as saying you're going to speak. And then he qualifies it by saying "by such means as are within my reach", which half undoes the speaking. I'm not putting that very well. And that word "reach" –'

'You're putting it splendidly. What about "reach"?'

'It's a word for contact, for one person reaching out to another, crossing the space between them rather than doing something to them. And then, "You pierce my soul." He tries to cross the space between them, and she – she goes through his soul, yet the words are so abstract, so lacking in any sense of substance, that it's like light passing through a window.'

'This beautiful place, and the lovely summer's afternoon, seem to be doing something to *your* soul. You are seeing some things in the text which I've never noticed.'

'Reading things in that aren't there, I expect.'

'The words say what they say, S, and you are reading them, perhaps as carefully and accurately as Anne will read Frederick's letter. The reader has to listen intently to the words of a letter such as this. It requires slow reading rather than the fast reading skills which seem to be in vogue.'

'So… the meaning isn't to be thought of as something which the writer constructs and then somehow aims at the reader. It's more a process to which each contributes half.'

'Just as Frederick is half agony, half hope. Which of the two is in him and which seems to come from Anne will no doubt change from moment to moment. Yes, nothing is being *done to* the reader here. And the writer seems to say that that kind of communication, where the speaker gives and the listener reacts – warning, commanding, that sort of thing – isn't to the point here.'

'He says "Tell me not". I see. Do you really think Jane Austen intended us to analyse it as closely as this?'

'Perhaps she didn't have intentions for us in that sense.'

'Because that would mean she was trying to bring about an effect, make us do something, as if we had no part of our own to play in reading her?'

'Something like that.'

'And we've only looked at the first few lines! Look, further on in the letter even identity begins to collapse – he offers himself, he says, but he is already hers, so not strictly himself, not *his* self. And she nearly did something to him, to his heart, which was hers, but didn't quite – break it. Then, "I have loved none but you." That simple sentence has such force after what has gone before.'

'It seems to reassert their separate and familiar identities after the metaphysical complexities that have gone before!'

'I'm not sure about "metaphysical", but I think I see what you mean. And then we're back to interpenetration again. He can't imagine she has failed to understand his wishes, he has been trying to read her feelings, she has penetrated his feelings.'

'And after he has said he can hardly write – that business which looks so one-way, so replete with the possibility of techniques of effectiveness – he shows so clearly that he is a listener, someone who can pick out Anne's voice – her particular quality or register, we might say – even at its softest. At the very end he is the attentive listener again, straining to interpret "a word, a look".'

'He says he's "uncertain", too. The rhythm of the language seems to tell us that. Throughout the words rush, then stop, sentences seem to break down even when the grammar is all right.'

'Mind you, he does offer her assurances of Security – no, I'm not laughing at you. "True attachment and constancy among men". And wasn't there a "Durable" in your acronym? "Dare not say that man forgets sooner than woman, that his love has an earlier death." You could say too that the letter enacts a high degree of intimacy between Frederick and Anne, that it is a promise of enhanced performance to come!'

'Please don't. That seems altogether the wrong sort of language for what we have been reading.'

'Then how shall we sum it up? That communication worth having – some of it at the very least – is about openness, tentativeness, attentiveness, mutuality? About sensitivity to words and the rhythms of sentences? About the way words and sentences seem to do a kind of dance together? What else shall we say?'

'I'd rather we didn't try to sum it up at all.'

(Nor do we want to sum up what has been going here, except to note that much of the conversation between S and T has exhibited many of the qualities of the letter they have been reading. They too have been highly attentive, to each other's words as well as to Jane Austen's, and to the words behind the words: the irony, for example, the occasional sardonic flash, the real warmth of appreciation and the pleasure of sharing something worth sharing. These things are not a matter of 'effective communication' and they cannot happen like this with information technology, even of the most interactive sort. Nor can the strategic pauses and silences, the careful interruption to focus on a particular idea; above all the *listening* that is needed to see when a growing insight can be fostered, when it needs to be reflected for clarification, when a sense of pleasure needs to be celebrated. They cannot happen in large lectures, unless the lecturer is spectacularly gifted. Even then, perhaps, it is not the same kind of thing.)

'So how would you write to your young woman now, S? Supposing that there really was one, and supposing – what I now find hard to believe – that you didn't have the confidence to talk with her directly. I can't help thinking too that there seem to be some strange assumptions underlying the whole business. Let me ask you: of all the qualities you would look for in a girlfriend or partner, what would you put first?'

'That's easy – everyone knows that "gsoh", good sense of humour, comes out on top in all the lonely hearts advertisements!'

'True. And people seem often to like to form relationships with people who are a little vulnerable, people whom they can care for. But you said, I think, that we like people who've got something going for them, or words to that effect. As if success and material things were what really counted in personal relationships.'

'Well, survival of the fittest, I suppose.'

'Yet "fittest" here turns out to include vulnerability and a good sense of humour, and not the rather forceful qualities that talk of "the fittest" usually makes us think of.'

'That's odd, I agree. But survival of the fittest holds good in general, doesn't it? I mean, if our university doesn't attract students then it won't survive. And don't you academics get ranked on how much you research and write – "publish or perish"? Which reminds me of something I've meant to ask you before, but I wasn't sure if you'd mind.'

'If it seems all right to you to talk about asking it, then I'm sure it's all right to ask it!'

'It's just that you don't seem to have written very much. I mean, if you type in Professor L's name in the library search there's page after page of it. I know you wrote that book about fifteen years ago, and I think there's some articles... I mean, don't you have to write more, don't you want to?'

'"I can hardly write. I am every instant hearing something which over-powers me." Sorry: the pull of *Persuasion* again. Seriously, often I feel I'm too busy hearing, or reading, things which overpower me. Just in the last year I've come across several novelists, a number of poets and some philosophical writing which completely stunned me. Which do you think would help me be a better teacher: to read more, and be impressed by much of what I read, and want to share it with my students, or to write some more articles for academic journals, and then rewrite them and put them together to make a book or two? I'm not wholly opposed to the assessment of writing and research. It's a good excuse to avoid administration, for a start, if there's pressure on to do research. And another thing: when I came into university life 20 years ago, there was a kind of unofficial pecking order of departments here, which owed more to longevity and snobbery than anything else. In the first Research Assessment Exercise some very complacent and well-regarded depart-ments scored very low indeed, and it did the university no end of good. So two cheers for the assessment of research But not three, because the whole thing is threatening to get out of hand. Sheer quantity, whatever the technical restrictions of the Research Assessment Exercise, carries much more weight than it ought.

'It's very valuable to write a book or some articles when you are trying to make your intellectual position clear, to yourself as much as anyone else, or when some genuine research needs to be put into the public domain so it can be evaluated and tested, or when some downright nonsense needs to be countered. But now most of us do it out of panic. Do you know, my department regularly circulates a document listing who has written what, who has got what research money, who has been where and given a conference paper, since the last document came round. It makes you feel inadequate even if you've been there, done this, written that. I recently found myself at Amsterdam airport en route for Hong Kong thinking "this will look good, anyway". When I found myself thinking that, I felt so ashamed I nearly turned round and came back.'

'I thought that was one of the few perks of being an academic – jetting around to conferences at someone else's expense!'

'Only if you take David Lodge's novels too literally. And of course often when you publish something in an academic journal there's hardly a sign that anyone ever reads it – unless you put it on student reading lists and make them, and some might say there was an ethical problem about that, and certainly about making your books compulsory texts. Then too, once the words are down on the page you never know what people will make of them. This is a particular problem if you write with an ironic twist, indeed if you do anything other than write in the most prosaic and direct way. I have it on good authority that some things I have written have been taken entirely at their face value by some of their readers.'

'So you think that the real work of the university is teaching, not writing. Or at least that the writing should somehow be in the service of the teaching.'

'Let me put it this way. Yesterday I arrived early for my Essay Skills class. It was a hot day, and many of the seminar room doors were open to let the air circulate. What do you think I saw going on in all those seminars?'

'If it's like most of my seminars, I think I know what you found. In virtually every one the tutor, the seminar leader, was doing all the talking, and had turned it into a mini-lecture. Perhaps there was just one or two where a student had been told to prepare a paper, and they were still droning on while everyone else went to sleep.'

'So that's business as usual, is it? That's exactly what I found. Nowhere any dialogue, arguing, questioning, no laughter or passion of any kind. I passed down the corridor, and found rooms full of students sitting silently in front of computer screens. And I reflected that most of these students would have come from lectures, where they sat and listened and hoped to come out with a good set of notes. Sometimes, S, I think that words have died in the university, and all we have is the desiccated ghosts of them fluttering about like the shades in Homer's underworld. We don't know how to breathe life into them, whether in our teaching or our writing. Dead committee prose, dead lectures, dead articles, dead essays in which "the present writer inclines to the view that, on the basis of the evidence reviewed" – because some herder of ghosts told her she was never to put the word "I" in a piece of academic writing.'

'There are debating societies – '

'Social occasions where you gawp at the famous visiting speaker. Language on stilts, and everyone quoting Dr Johnson and Oscar Wilde. Ghosts in dinner jackets. Sorry, tuxedos.'

'Is there no hope for the modern university, then? Isn't there going to be some new thing called an Institute for Learning and Teaching, which trains lecturers in how to teach? It strikes me that some of your col-leagues, if I may say so, would benefit from learning how to run semi-nars, how to ask open questions, how to encourage people by not criticizing their answers immediately, how it's a good idea to try to learn students' names or even tell them what their own name is! If that's come out a little pat, probably it's because it's something else that Professor L was talking about this morning. He was very critical of the level of com-munication skills amongst academics.'

'Then he and I have a great deal more in common than I thought. Though I might want to add a few things that he probably would not. For instance, it's often forgotten that good teaching requires a degree of courage. If you let your students argue with you, for example, they will often win! Some people find what you called a mini-lecture much safer. So you have to find all kinds of ways of encouraging people to take risks, and that isn't something that the present climate encourages at all. Also to be a good teacher you have to quite like your students, or at least most of them on most days, and no one likes to mention that because it sounds sentimental at best and at worst you might get accused of favouritism or sexual harassment.

'As for an Institute for Learning and Teaching in Higher Education, it is such a promising idea that I dread to see it become what I fear it will: another body which is really concerned with accreditation and certifica-tion rather than the tricky business of human relationships, growing up, making mistakes, talking to each other and sharing the pain and plea-sure of learning together; with "words written on the soul of the hearer to enable him to learn about the right, the beautiful and the good". No, not Jane Austen: Plato.'

'Talking of Jane Austen, T, what happened to – what was his name? – Frederick Wentworth? Did he get his woman?'

'If you read *Persuasion* with that question in mind, and if you keep your eye on how books, letters and writing come into the story, you will gain a great deal more pleasure than if I scratch your momentary itch of curios-ity! This place under the tree has done us well, but we hardly need the shade now that the sun is going down. May your communication skills increase, S, but, more than that, may you use them as sensitively as you do effectively. Now we both of us have to move on. Shall we go?'

Does this kind of thing ever happen any more, supposing that it ever did? Should it happen? The potential for sheer self-indulgence, as well as for the other dangers that T mentions, is clearly there. There are, then, risks. But sometimes perhaps risks ought to be taken, and there seems to be some truth in the idea that real learning – learning that touches people and changes their lives a little – does not occur unless some of the barriers and defences come down. Here T makes little attempt to hide behind the professional persona of 'academic.' He reveals something about himself, his life and his deepest commitments. He shows *what university education can mean for a life*. If there is to be talk of higher education being 'life-enhancing', then here is one performance indicator which T is meeting rather well. (And surely, T, no one will miss the irony in that!)

Perhaps this is the point to shed some of our own disembodiedness, and emerge a little from behind our triple anonymity. One of us (at least) had the good luck to have several tutors like T: men (again we acknowledge that there is a gender issue here that we have not explored) who invited you to their house for Sunday lunch, and held seminars in pubs and on river-banks and in other unlikely places, and who one day in May took five undergraduates for a long, hot walk to ensure they had one day away from their books, were thoroughly tired and had a good night's sleep, a week before their final examinations. Through them I learnt something of what university education can mean for a life, and I am grateful.

Lastly, some readers may notice resemblances between the story of S and T and Plato's dialogue, the *Phaedrus*. Like our characters, Socrates and Phaedrus meet each other outside the city and walk by a river-bank. Like them, they discuss personal relationships, communication and learning. And with Socrates and Phaedrus too there seems to be something in the nature of the relationship between teacher and taught rather warmer and more lively than anything in the pages of Dearing or, it must be said, in almost anything written these days about higher education in the academic style. (The novelists, of course, are different.) In that dialogue, although Socrates is supposedly the teacher and Phaedrus the student, each seems to learn a little more about himself, partly through finding himself reflected to some extent in the person of the other. Martha Nussbaum, in her illuminating commentary, finds there the two Muses, of philosophy and poetry, working together,

> combining the rigor of speculative argument with sensitive responses to the particulars of human experience. It demands from us a boldness, and a freedom from set ideas, in our own response... The whole thing is a Music discourse, which asks of us the full participation of all parts of our souls. (Nussbaum, 1986: 227)

That would be a high aim for university education, but it is the nature of an ideal to be high.

References

Anderson, J (1980) *Education and Inquiry*, D Z Phillips (ed), Blackwell, Oxford

Barnett, R (1992) *Improving Higher Education: Total Quality Care*, Open University Press for SRHE, Buckingham

Barnett, R (1994) *The Limits of Competence*, Open University Press, Buckingham

Barnett, R (1997a) *Realizing the University*, Institute of Education University of London, London

Barnett, R (1997b) 'Beyond competence', in Coffield and Williamson (1997)

Blackstone, T (1997a) 'Open all hours for the masses', *The Times Higher Education Supplement*, 17 October 1997

Blackstone, T (1997b) 'Ability to pay tops the bill', *Guardian Higher Education*, 2 December 1997, p iii

Blake, N (1998) 'Industrial innovation, local identity, and higher education: a democratic response to globalisation', in Crawley *et al*, (1998)

Blake, N, Smeyers, P, Smith, R and Standish, P (1998) *Thinking Again: Education after Postmodernism*, Bergin & Garvey, Westport, Connecticut and London

Cantwell, J (1995) 'Innovation in a global world', *New Economy*, 2:2, 66–70

Cave, M, Hanney, S, Henkel, M and Kogan, M (1997) *The Use of Performance Indicators in Higher Education*, Jessica Kingsley, London

Coffield, F and Williamson, W (eds) (1997), *Repositioning Higher Education*, Open University Press, Buckingham

CPVE (1985) Joint Board Unit for the Business and Technical Education Council (B/TEC) and City and Guilds of London Institute, London

Crawley, F, Smeyers, P and Standish, P (eds) (1998, forthcoming) *Remembering Europe: Nations, Culture, and Higher Education*, Berghahn, Oxford

CSUP (1992) *Teaching and Learning in an Expanding Higher Education System*, CSUP, Edinburgh

CVCP (1998) 'CVCP position statement: Assuring standards and enhancing quality', 8 May, http://wwwcvcpacuk/pubs/positionhtml

Dewey, J (1937) 'Democracy and educational administration', *School and Society* 45:1162

Dunne, J (1993) *Back to the Rough Ground: 'Phronesis' and 'Techne' in Modern Philosophy and in Aristotle*, University of Notre Dame Press, Illinois

Emerson, R W (1985) *Selected Essays*, Larzer Ziff (ed), Penguin Books, London

References

European Commission (1995) 'Teaching and learning: towards the learning society', European Commission, Website http://wwwceclu/en/comm/dg22/dgss/html, Brussels

Fielding, M (1998) 'The point of politics: friendship and community in the work of John Macmurray', *Renewal*, 6:1, 55–64

Fryer, R H (1997) *Learning for the Twenty-First Century*, First report of the National Advisory Group for Continuing Education and Lifelong Learning

Fuller, T (ed) (1989) *The Voice of Liberal Learning: Michael Oakeshott on Education*, Yale University Press, New Haven

Gibbs, G (1992) *Improving the Quality of Student Learning*, Technical and Educational Services, Bristol

Glennerster, H (1991) 'Quasi-markets for education?', *Economic Journal*, 101

Gray, J (1998) *False Dawn: The Delusions of Global Capitalism*, Granta, London

Group for Continuing Education and Lifelong Learning, edited and abridged version in *THES*, 28 November 1997

Habermas, J (1978) *Knowledge and Human Interests*, Heinemann, London

Hart, W A (1997) 'The qualitymongers', *Journal of Philosophy of Education*, 31:2, 295–308

Hillman, J (1996) *University for Industry: Creating a National Learning Network*, London: IPPR

Hillman, J (1998) 'The Labour government and lifelong learning', *Renewal*, 6:2, 63–72

Kamenka, E (1980) 'Anderson on education and academic freedom', in Anderson, (1980)

Kennedy, H (1997) *Learning Works: Widening Participation in Further Education* (The Kennedy Report), The Further Education Funding Council, Coventry

Kuhn, T (1962) *The Structure of Scientific Revolutions*, University of Chicago Press, Chicago

Larmore, C (1987) *Patterns of Moral Complexity*, Cambridge University Press, Cambridge

MacIntyre, A (1980) *After Virtue*, Duckworth, London

MacIntyre, A (1990) *Three Rival Versions of Moral Enquiry*, Duckworth, London

Macmurray, J (1929) *The Kingdom of Heaven*, Sermon preached at Balliol College, Oxford, Sunday 19 May, Oxonian Press, Oxford

Macmurray, J (1941a) 'Two lives in one', *Listener*, 36:675, 18 December, p 822

Macmurray, J (1941b) 'The community of mankind', *Listener* 36:675, 24 December, p 856

Macmurray, J (1961) *Persons in Relation*, Faber, London

Medawar, P B (1968), 'Lucky Jim', in Watson (1981)

Morgan, A (1993) *Improving Your Students' Learning: Reflections on the experience of study*, Kogan Page, London

National Committee of Inquiry into Higher Education (The Dearing Report) (1997) HMSO, London

Nussbaum, M (1986) *The Fragility of Goodness*, Cambridge University Press, Cambridge

Nussbaum, M (1990) *Love's Knowledge: Essays on Philosophy and Literature*, Oxford University Press, Oxford

Pahl, R and Spencer, L (1997) 'The politics of friendship', *Renewal*, 5:3 & 4, 100–107

Pelikan, J (1992) *The Idea of the University: A reexamination*, Yale University Press, New Haven and London

QAA (The Quality Assurance Agency for Higher Education) (1998) *Higher Quality*, 3:1, QAA, London

Reynolds, D and Teddlie, C (eds) (1997) *The International Handbook on School Effectiveness Research*, Falmer, London

Richardson, H S (1997) *Practical Reasoning about Final Ends*, Cambridge University Press, Cambridge

Robertson, D (1994) *Choosing to Change: Education, Access, Choice and Mobility in Higher Education*, Higher Education Funding Council, London

Robertson, D (1996) 'Paying for learning', *New Economy*, Autumn, 154–157

Robertson, D (1997) 'Social justice in a learning market', in Coffield and Williamson (1997)

Robinson, P (1998) *The Tyranny of League Tables*, IPPR, London

School Curriculum and Assessment Authority (SCAA) (1996) *Education for Adult Life: the Spiritual and Moral Development of Young People* (Discussion Paper 6), School Curriculum and Assessment Authority, London

Schrag, F (1995) *Back to Basics*, Jossey-Bass, San Francisco

Smith, R and Standish, P (1997) *Teaching Right and Wrong: Moral Education in the Balance*, Trentham Books, Stoke-on-Trent

Standish, P (1991) 'Educational discourse: meaning and myth', *Journal of Philosophy of Education*, 25:2, 171–182

Watson, J D (1981) *The Double Helix: A Personal Account of the Discovery of the Structure of DNA*, Gunther S Stent (ed), Weidenfield and Nicholson, London

Williams, B (1985) *Ethics and the Limits of Philosophy*, Fontana, London

Index of Names